Word Articulatio

For Te

The Word Wasp

Phonics and Structure
A Manual for Teaching the Rules and Structures of English
(Reading and Spelling)

Harry Cowling & Marie Cowling

III

First published in the year 2000 by
H J Cowling
Pudsey, West Yorkshire

Pilot Impression	July	2000	
First Edition	October	2000	ISBN 0-9538714-0-1
Second Edition	December	2003	ISBN 0-9538714-1-X
Third Edition	September	2007	ISBN 0-9538714-3-6

Revised Third Edition: Published by Harry and Marie Cowling December 2011

IV

Photocopying

People cite any number of reasons for poor literacy skills. They are a matter of complete
indifference to the individual with the problem. For these people, the problem is deeply personal.
The Word Wasp is a tool for the individual student. It is an unassuming text which teaches literacy skills
without recourse to patronising gimmicks and childish graphics. It is for those students who aspire
to sit alongside their literate peers and share the same opportunities without drawing undue attention
to their struggle. The Word Wasp is their record of achievement. Some students will learn faster than
others therefore it is a necessary requirement that each individual has their own book.

Experience has also revealed that many teachers take it upon themselves to form ad hoc programmes,
using parts of one programme in the hope that it will complement another. The Word Wasp stands on its
own and its effects will be diminished and not strengthened by photocopying.

Photocopying will not be permitted under any circumstances.

Coaching begins on page 20

Acknowledgements

Marie Dickinson was the first student to complete the draft Toe by Toe and has now become the most careful, resourceful, patient and totally committed literacy coach. She is now called Cowling which pleases me enormously but may drive her to an early grave! Thanks for the support, the wisdom, the love and now: the advice!

Elaine Watts was one of the first to recognize the WASP's potential and she became a dedicated coach, friend, and organiser of the Crawshaw School trials. Without Elaine's organisational skills and commitment, our trials would have been greatly reduced and much more difficult to maintain. Thanks Elaine!

Val Miller, UWCN, overturned the stone under which I had been hiding and thrust me into the glaring light of her students' attentions. Many thanks Val. You were brilliant! So here's a toast to yellow wellies, weak bladders, and white-knuckle rides.

"If one tells the truth, one is sure, sooner or later, to be found out."
Oscar Wilde

VI

The Real Alternatives

Nothing in life was gained without struggle. We are born in dialectical opposition to nature. We struggle to live.

Literacy is a weapon we use to understand and deal with the world in which we live. Learning our language is no different to learning any other skill. There are conceptual thresholds to cross. Some students will cross those thresholds without much difficulty; others will require a modest amount of assistance; others may require huge amounts. All students have the right to be taught English by the rules and structures which operate the language. We do not have the right to condemn students with literacy problems to learn a service language which will do little more than allow them to fill in a form or sign a cheque!

Reluctant students, who have been subject to whole-word techniques, have been deluded into thinking that those teachers who subscribe to 'alternative' methodologies; based on word frequency; whole-word and multi-sensory methods; have also learned by those methods. Nothing could be further from the truth! A literacy problem can be defined as the lack of familiarity with the rules and structures of the language. How can we address such problems by ignoring them?

Students with literacy problems are sick of feeling inferior and sick of being patronised. They are on the road to alienation from both school and society in general and with good reason! Teachers too, at all levels, suffer as a result. The alienation felt by many students is creating conditions where education and school are becoming mutually exclusive entities. It is in the interest of both teachers and students that the teaching of English, unfettered by governmental interference, using the rules and structures of the language should be returned to the heart of the curriculum.

As a first step: Special Needs Education should be dealt with as a curriculum subject and not something on the fringes whereby unruly students are minded whilst they pass through the educational system. The real alternatives to crime, poverty, war and social strife are gained through education. H.G. Wells in his 'Outline of History' makes the point that "Human history becomes more and more a race between education and catastrophe." In this race 'education' appears to have been seriously handicapped by illiteracy.

Structure or Word Recognition

Teaching children to read and spell successfully is a rewarding experience. Teaching adults to read and spell successfully is both rewarding and enlightening. Children are often overawed by the presence of adults and often too stigmatized by past failure to express their doubts or ask questions.

My most earnest efforts to teach children and adults to spell met with limited short term success, as did my attempts to teach dyslexic students a limited Shakespearean experience through word analysis and word recognition exercises.

One element of the teaching methods employed to achieve that partial success was phonics. It was particularly successful with adults. Children also, seemed easier to handle when they were dealing with structures.

Teachers of literacy will be all too familiar with the infectious yawns of struggling children. Word-building was less likely to stimulate the nose-picking, yawning and general mayhem of other methods and gradually, in my private teaching, I began to place more emphasis on word building than other methods. Earlier, under guidance from others considered at the time to be experts, I taught spelling by any means available: mnemonics, rhymes, over-teaching and finger tracing. Those methods were all about memorizing and recognizing generically unrelated words.

When it came to teaching someone particularly close, an adult member of my own family, I was allowed for the first time to concentrate solely on the structure of the language with as much time as was necessary. The results were astounding. Using nothing other than phonetics and rules my student advanced at a rate so fast that I feared the effects would be psychologically damaging. However, although my student's reading age advanced dramatically, the same success could not be matched by my teaching of spelling although spelling had been improved generally as a result of the word-building.

The writing and testing of Toe by Toe had led to an impasse: Phonics and structure was the fuel which propelled my student to a level of decoding which I had thought unachievable but Toe by Toe the classroom system was not entirely based on Phonics and structure. By far the largest system was based on a whole-word methodology particularly the spelling.

The common complaint from my student was: "I'm running out of room." Ignoring these apposite remarks, even more complex mnemonics were applied and they were used more frequently. It wasn't until my struggle to remember the mnemonic which I had been using to teach a certain word became embarrassing that the total futility of the strategy became clear: a small dictionary can contain over 70,000 entries! Finally my student, in the face of my doubts, insisted that I attempt to teach her to spell by the same method that had taught her to read. It worked and the results were phenomenal. Not only did she learn to spell her decoding

also improved dramatically. Teaching spelling in isolation from reading doesn't work. **W**ord **A**rticulation **S**pelling and **P**ronunciation form the integrated structure of our language. They cannot be taught successfully in isolation from each other.

History and Structure

Our language has developed over several thousand years. It is the means whereby we communicate the structures and meaning of speech to others, in the absence of the speakers of that language, through written symbols. In spite of the diverse cultural, social and national origins of our language, its structures follow rules which must be learned before we can communicate in written form. The building blocks of any language has to be the 'sounds'. The mortar which binds them are the rules; a knowledge of grammar allows us to become the architects of communication. The basic sounds are organized in our alphabet; we then construct further sounds by combining letters which broadens the sound base of our communication. We push and weave them together to form words.

Special needs teachers will have noticed that many children with weak literacy skills can be remarkably proficient at playing draughts or chess or using construction sets. There are others too traumatised and alienated by their misery to show any expression other than anxiety or disruptive behaviour.

The moves of the court pieces on a chess board can be likened to the action of vowels in our language. Why is it then, that many people believe that we cannot teach the construction of English spelling by the rules of the language itself? Why is it supposed that the shape of a word is more important than the structural order of the sounds and rules that formed it?

This text's approach to literacy begins and ends with the sounds and rules of English spelling and reading. There is a small place for other methods but they play a very minor role in the teaching of exceptions and only when the broader range of spelling and reading has been taught. Those students who finish this text will have their spelling ages and as a consequence, their reading ages, advanced dramatically.

There were those amongst the Special Needs establishment who would have thrown up their hands in horror and suggested that our programme was too

pedagogic and structured. Thankfully, the rise of phonics has swept away even those with feet mired in the post-Plowden clay.

The Word Wasp is about English and the application of its structures and rules. It owes no allegiance to any other purported method of teaching other than those which stem from the language itself. It deems all students equal. It makes no distinctions. Some students, particularly those who have been taught to read through word recognition techniques, will be slower to start than others. Some students fear this text because their supplies of self-esteem have been exhausted through years of failure. No one student will learn at the same rate as another but all will learn and learn well.

The Development of The Word Wasp and Special Educational Needs

Our confidence in The Word Wasp arises not only from our own experience of using it but from the experience of others who have used it with both adults and children. Housewives, electricians, print workers and students have been test coaches for The Word Wasp. This is a method developed for the kitchen table so that it will complement special educational needs in school. Specialist training is not needed. Classroom assistants and parents can use this book successfully.

Good spelling skills cannot be acquired by memorising lists of unrelated words. Older students provide us with an inexhaustible supply of horror stories concerning lists of words to be spelled by Monday mornings. Detentions and other punishments were one price of failure; ridicule and shame were others. One student revealed how she laboured over spellings every weekend and always managed to achieve the acceptable level of eight out of ten until the teacher, for the sake of perversity, decided to ask the spellings in reverse order. She failed miserably to spell all but two correctly.

Encoding Teaches Decoding

The Word Wasp begins by teaching students to spell (encode) simple sounds. It never ceases to amaze me that so many students, adults included, cannot spell the basic sounds of our language. From simple sounds it moves to simple words. Many students spell only that which they hear and many sounds are barely audible. The word 'ducts' will be heard as 'ducks' by those with weak literacy skills because the final letters are blended into one amorphous sound. The Word Wasp emphasizes every letter and coaches will be taught to articulate words for spelling.

Students are invited to read (decode) words and passages in order that they can see, hear, and build the structures and rules of our language and make a necessary link between spelling and speech. If a student is able to spell the word then they acquire a stronger grip on the printed word. Words become so much easier to read.

The rules which operate the words in our language are introduced in gradual steps and each step is woven into the structure through the various exercises. The mechanisms for teaching the spelling of difficult words are constantly repeated. Good spelling cannot be achieved without some knowledge of basic grammar. The difference between the incorrect spelling 'riskt' and 'risked' is the knowledge of simple past tense.

The Word Wasp teaches all these skills slowly and carefully. The pronunciation columns and passages do not contain every skill. It is not presumed that every skill needs to be taught. This text provides a springboard for literacy. Hundreds of words will be learned directly as a result of using this text: significantly more than those now discredited methods which relied on memory training techniques.

The Word Wasp invites students to look for the patterns in our language. These patterns are learned as they become confident with a language which to them has always appeared as a frustrating enigma.

To those who say that students cannot be taught by the rules; the reply must be that students were taught by the rules for centuries and if you don't know the rules then its high time you learned them.
To those who say that The Word Wasp is teaching students to "bark at print" the reply is this:

Students of The Word Wasp will ask what a word means and not ask what it says. Students of The Word Wasp learn both reading and spelling skills. The Word Wasp gives students the tools for the job!

Before using The Word Wasp your student will have believed that every word had a unique structure and pattern. They will have poor reading skills by comparison with others. Many will have struggled against impossible odds to achieve a sustainable level of literacy: a level which has given them a crumb of credibility in a world of literate people, but that level of literacy will not remove the fear of being 'discovered'. That fear and the ignorance

which so often accompanies it are the enemies that The Word Wasp aims to destroy.

This is an angry little book but not quite as angry as it once was!

Harry Cowling 2011

The Development of the Third Edition

Marie Cowling has been a vital part of the Word Wasp since its creation but it is in this latest edition that Marie has had her greatest input. Marie's dedicated coaching of students and continuous drive to enhance the text's practical application has resulted in this latest edition being much the best by far.

Since the book's publication, she has been responsible for organizing the largest of our coaching trials using both the Wasp and the Hornet Literacy Primer with upper school students with a variety of problems and all with substantially lower reading ages than their chronological ages. We were at hand to monitor progress and administer tuition alongside teaching assistants and sixth form volunteers.

In addition to monitoring the trials, we have been able to look more critically at the performance of our coaches. That which we observed did not always fill us with unbridled joy. Progress varied but, nevertheless, progress was made.

The requirements of the school and those of the National Curriculum had to be considered above every other concern: even when a student's literacy skills were so scant that they were not discernible, they were expected to be present at a modern language class.

Students were not selected for their positive attitudes. Negative behaviour, which often stems from frustration, was ever present. We were allowed one hour a week to coach some extremely difficult students; some with six year lags between chronological and reading age. However, the single, most difficult problem to overcome was the patronizing attitudes of some of our coaches. It is a problem endemic in Special Needs Education where 'Needs' are rarely identified or addressed. There are bridges to cross which are not even approached because it is easier to patronize than it is to respect.

One coach was discovered applauding a student every time a word was read or spelled correctly. Other coaches adopted psuedo-empathetic attitudes; doodling in the margins of the text and allowing students to dictate the structure and progress made. The general complaint was that many coaches were treating these upper school students as infants. Students may be happy, hostile, alienated, enthusiastic, friendly or antagonistic: infants they are not!

We were expecting coaches to read instructions but that was rarely the case. We also realized that the instructions, in some cases, were little more than adequate and many coaches admitted to learning the rules alongside their students, which is acceptable, but it leads to situations whereby the student's needs are not realized until the coach becomes familiar with the rules. That problem is ameliorated when a coach takes on another student but it makes for tough going in a large scale trial. All but a small minority of our students were allotted just one hour per week for Wasp coaching. Remove time for absences, holidays, truancies, staffing problems and general hostilities; the actual time for implementing the programme was ridiculously short.

With just two experienced coaches to teach, organize and monitor large numbers of students and coaches; it was an extremely difficult trial to launch. Added to the problem was that of absences and departures, as a result of which, many coaches were pitched, unwillingly, into the middle of a text; often without the experience of the beginning! However, progress was made. Independent monitoring of the trial revealed that even the worst coaches were capable of making significant advances and in some cases the progress could be described as astonishing.

All our coaches are improving as they teach and many, if not all, would describe the experience as enlightening.

The seemingly intractable problems encountered when coaching difficult students led to the trial of new strategies. The solutions and necessary strategies have now been encompassed by the new edition. They have also given us the experience and relevant data to produce a new text.

The Hornet Literacy Primer

Like the Wasp, the Hornet eschews patronising and insensitive graphics and again, like the Wasp, it can be used by parents alone or in conjunction with school literacy programmes. It can be used with younger children and adults alike. It has a low threshold and a slow start.

Marie has been desperate to avoid the spotlight but she has constructed many of the new exercises and provided most of the enthusiasm.

Marie's influence has been critical in the development, structure, writing and editing of both the Hornet and the Wasp. Her name joins mine where it belongs: on the cover.

H J C 2011

Vespula Lexica Vulgaris

The Common Word Wasp

Coaching Begins on Page 20

Crawshaw School

The Word Wasp has been used at Crawshaw School Pudsey West Yorks, since September 2000. The results have been astonishing! The Author and his wife Marie have headed a diverse coaching team which includes two students formerly diagnosed as 'severely dyslexic'. The other coaches are all Non - Teaching Assistants.

The Word Wasp has made a real difference at Crawshaw School and I have no hesitation in recommending its use as a corrective programme to support student's basic literacy skills.

For several years, The Word Wasp has been used successfully with a full range of students with learning difficulties. All the students working with Harry and Marie's team have made huge gains in their reading and spelling abilities.

It is fantastic to see them working with our students; putting their own system into practice. Their belief in the merits of Word Wasp are fully supported by our own SENCO and teaching assistants who have also used the system in school.

Nigel Turner Head Teacher

The students have ranged from dyslexic to those with Asperger's Syndrome. I've been astounded by the progress made. Everything is improving: articulation, spelling and reading! Confidence has been raised and they are coping much better both in the classroom and with their peers. The manual looks and feels adult and doesn't demean them in anyway. One Word Wasp student is now using the Wasp to teach her mum!

Phil Jackson M. Ed (Senco/Advanced Skills Teacher)

XVI

Coach

Learning language forms part of the struggle to deal with, and understand, the world around us. Make no mistake: the struggle you are about to undertake is, possibly, the most important one of your student's life.

If your student has been used to failure then this book represents 'fear'. Students will not be aware that this system is any different from the useless, patronizing garbage to which students with literacy problems are routinely subjected. Such students can only presume that their teachers were taught by the same useless methods. They can only ask themselves the introspective question: 'What's so different about me?' They may already believe that they are failures with a genetic predisposition for failure. You are about to destroy that myth

Illiteracy is not a disease and therefore there is no miracle cure. Literacy is a low grade skill the teaching of which has been neglected for decades. There will be struggles to teach certain concepts but, as yet, all our students have made spectacular progress. Some were harder to teach than others but every student advanced and found that they were not destined to be educationally unequal to others.

This text has been used with children and adults with the severest difficulties. Take confidence in the text: the rest is up to you. You will learn as you go. We will not wish you luck until the end because fortune will play no part in your student's journey. You will find difficulties. There will be frustration but there will be progress, and with progress: satisfaction and joy.

Bon Voyage!

Harry and Marie Cowling October 2008

A Last Word

Hopefully, this edition will no longer be another prototype and the process of refinement and adjustment will have resulted in the text that we have so desperately tried to create over the last 12 years. The methodology was of paramount concern in the earlier prototypes but then we had to concern ourselves with the delivery of the programme. There were many shortcomings but the overall strength of the methodology buoyed the programme significantly and the results we were getting at Crawshaw School buoyed the coaching team even higher.

Once the programme was launched, oiled and tweaked; we set about monitoring the coaches and found that our instructions were not as accessible as we thought and many of them needed to be expanded and made clearer. But we still made good progress!

The refinements and alterations have made this a much easier text to use and we have shifted the balance between decoding and encoding. We can now nail our colours to the mast: we teach students to spell but this was always going to be a manual to teach literacy. We were always ready to admit that we taught reading through spelling and **WASP** still stands for **Word Articulation Spelling and Pronunciation**. The code of our language involves decoding, encoding, assembly and delivery. These are not separable entities and we have the results to back our theories and methodology. The bulk of our students, not just those with 'Statements', when tested, did not have a discernible reading or spelling age. The Word Wasp programme dealt with them all successfully!

Pronunciation.

In the light of the trial at 'Crawshaw' which has processed a huge number of students through the WASP programme, we have used traditionally formed sounds with emphasis and not those sounds which APDUK presume to form part of sounds as they are formed in words. For hundreds, if not thousands, of years the extra emphasis has made sounds easier to recall. This method was dropped post Plowden, as was the teaching of phonics and the 'hissing whispers' approach was adopted. The results of this interference has left us with a massive literacy problem. Literacy was changed by Plowden and Warnock and the resulting catastrophe has still to be addressed.

The APDUK 'hissing whispers' approach, is an empirical answer which misses the point. Furthermore, and in total agreement with Professor Julian Elliot of Durham University, we believe that literacy is a low grade skill which has to be taught and the earlier and more intense the intervention; the easier it is to teach! 'Osmosis' and whole-word recognition methods are dead in the water and the 'hissing whispers' are neither lifelines nor lifeboats. Plowden and Warnock served a philosophy which upheld a policy of social engineering and fostered a service language suited to people who would not aspire to a fulfilled life. Under a banner of 'free expression' these people have become the disenfranchised; downwardly mobile prisoners of the class system which we were assured "no longer exists." That system is alive and flourishing and it will not budge until all our children are given the right of access to the rules and structures of our language. **Harry and Marie Cowling September 2008**

XVIII

Who Needs The Word Wasp?

Any individual with literacy problems including those diagnosed as dyslexic.

Is there a recommended age group? Our youngest student was eight years old; the oldest fifty-four. The Word Wasp is a structured system which requires all students, adults and children, to start with the basic letter sounds. It progresses from these sounds embracing a comprehensive range of complex words from 'lock' to 'loquacious'.

Is it possible for adults to miss out the early exercises? Definitely not! The Word Wasp is an integrated system; the foundations of which are the basic sound patterns of English. The exercises are linked from the beginning of the text to the end. Miss out any exercise and the result will be frustration.

Can anyone use The Word Wasp? The Word Wasp was designed for adults and children; utilizing the experiences of those adults who still remember the problems they encountered as children. The test coaches for The Word Wasp were not teachers. Housewives, office and factory workers, students and the unemployed have used The Word Wasp successfully. Parents and non-teaching assistants can use it without difficulty. Classroom assistants need only be monitored; leaving hard-pressed teaching staff to get on with other classroom business. Parents can use the book in conjunction with teaching staff.

What Do I Need?

1 A moderate ability to read the English Language.

2 Paper: A broad lined exercise book divided into columns. Narrow-lined paper inhibits the free movement of the hand and may result in the cultivation of an inhibited style. If your student's handwriting is particularly bad, then use two lines of a narrow lined paper: by taking every alternate line on the paper and going over it with a pencil line you will achieve a good broad writing line with a fainter guideline which will act as a marker for the lower case letters. The writing may be larger than is necessary but at least you should be able to read it. Better to scale good writing down than bad writing up! Always date the exercise sheets.

3 Pen / pencil? The ballpoint pen proliferates because they are cheap and readily available but they have never assisted the development of neat and legible handwriting. Fibre point tips break too easily. Legibility is crucial therefore an ordinary HB pencil is the best implement for the job.

4 Patience! Lots and lots of it! Be sympathetic but **never patronize**!

5 Read the instructions overleaf and then follow the coaching boxes throughout the text!

A lesson should begin with:

A student!
The Word Wasp
A lined exercise book
Scrap paper
A pencil
A pen
A table
Patience!

If your student is right-handed you must sit to his/her left in order that you can see the spellings as they are being written.

Corners are best but it is not an absolute necessity!

Reverse the positions for left-handed students. Wherever possible, you must try to see a word as it is being written. This is not always easy with left-handed students.

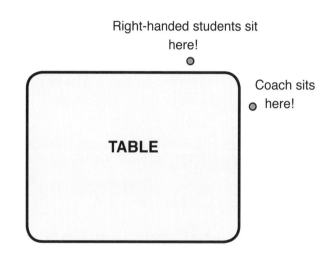

Right-handed students sit here!

Coach sits here!

TABLE

Preparation
Speaking for Spelling

A student with literacy problems has to rely on the vagaries of received sound; when coaches are reading words for spelling, it is vital that your student hears every syllable clearly before attempting to spell a particular sound or word.

Strategy:

The coach must look directly at the student as he/she reads the word or sound.

The student must be looking directly at the mouth of the coach.

The student must acknowledge that they have heard the sound or word by repeating it.

If the coach is satisfied that the student has heard the word correctly then the student may write the word or sound.

Students should be encouraged to spell out loud the sounds as they are being written. Remember! Sounds: '**a**' as in '**a**nt', '**b**' as in '**b**ag'.

Coaches who follow this process will be aware of any weakness immediately and will thus be able to correct and guide the student. It is important that the process of spelling and writing the sounds are simultaneous.

It will not take long for this process to become automatic.

Be aware of students who appear reluctant. Check that members of his or her peer group are not in the vicinity. It is vital that your student is familiar with the basic sounds of our language. It is not necessary to sacrifice a student's dignity in the process.

Hornet Students

Students who have completed the Hornet should start at the beginning: **page 29**. However, one tick is all that is required to complete elements of the exercise grids.

Should a Hornet student earn a dot, then and only then, and for that element, word/sound or sentence alone, are they required to earn two consecutive ticks. Continue marking in this manner until students reach the exercise on **page 92**; from there on, former Hornet students should be marked in the usual way: **two consecutive ticks (see pages 24 - 25)**.

Instructions: Marking the exercises

Look for two consecutive ticks (two together)!

Day	8	9	11	15	16	
Month	4	4	4	4	4	
Spell						
aft	/	·	/	·	/	unfinished
eft	/	·	/	/		completed
art	·	·	/	·	/	unfinished
oft	/	/				completed
gift	·	/	/			completed

The example **above** shows the pattern of ticks required before a student's spelling can be considered consistent enough to leave and move on. An exercise column has been completed when each word has two consecutive ticks. **The same instructions apply to the reading columns.** An exercise session begins by placing the date in the first column of the exercise grid. The example on the page **opposite** shows that the initial exercise began on August 2nd; continued on August 4th and then the 7th and 8th respectively. Place the date at the top of the column before you begin. Work down each dated column, **ticking or dotting** each word as required: a tick for a correct answer a dot for an incorrect answer. **Spelling or Pro (reading):** The words in the white **Pro** (reading) columns are for your student to read out loud; pronouncing each one in his/her normal manner of speech. The words in the blue **Spell** (spelling) columns are for the coach to read to his/her student. The student must then repeat the word, to ensure that they have heard the coach correctly, before writing the spelling. The blue background and italic print have been used to prevent easy visual access to the spellings.

How long should a lesson be?

Between twenty and forty minutes a session is usually enough. It isn't necessary to use the book on a daily basis but the more often you work with a student; the faster her/his progress will be. Much depends on your student's writing ability. Lined paper is preferable (**See page 20**).

Day	2	4	7	8
Month	8	8	8	8
Pro				
scr	/	·	/	/
shr	/	/		
squ	/	/		
squid	/	/		
spr	·	·	/	/
str	/	/		
spr	/	/		
sprig	/	/		
thrip	/	/		
split	/	/		

Day	2	4	7	8	9
Month	8	8	8	8	
Spell					
spot	/	/			
skin	/	/			
brag	/	/			
~~brim~~					
bliss	/	/			
dross	/	/			
cram	/	/			
fret	/	/			
slush	·	/	·	/	/
throb	/	/			

Day	2	4	7
Month	8	8	8
Spell			
brat	/	/	
thrift	·	/	/
smog	/	/	
blend	/		
strap	/	/	
splash	·	/	/
grip	/	/	
strip	/	/	
glass	/	/	
thrash	/	/	

Day	2	4	7	8
Month	8	8	8	8
Spell				
croft	/	/		
smug	/	/		
twist	/	/		
twill	/	/		
bless	/	/		
flesh	/	/		
flash	/	·	/	/
struck	/	/		
shred	/	/		
split	/	/		

Do not attempt the same column twice in the same day: one attempt for one tick or dot!

Never allow a student to start columns that he/she will be unable to finish before the end of the lesson.   A longhand script (joined-up writing) is preferable to printing but if the coach is unable to read the spellings then the student must print the words. The coach needs the book, some scrap paper and a pen; the student needs a pencil and lined paper.

Coach

Sounds are Vital!

Only the most unenlightened coaches still believe that their students do not need to learn the letter sounds on the opposite page. Those coaches will fail and their students will suffer as a consequence. Early failures, particularly with adults, stemmed from the notion that these basic sounds had made their way into a student's intellect by 'osmosis'. Describing them as 'baby sounds' fosters the belief that they form part of a genetic development, much like the development of milk teeth. Nothing could be further from the truth. Avoid presuming anything about a student's early development.

Vowel sounds are highlighted in green print. The sounds are: 'a' as in 'ant', 'b' as in 'bag', 'd' as in 'dog'. These sounds form the foundation blocks of our language. **Use the grid on the opposite page to establish the correct sound**.

Vowel names **only,** are highlighted in red print. Students must be made aware of the difference between vowel sounds and vowel names only.

Upper case vowels (capitals) are not entitled to say their name any more than lower case vowels!

The 'x' will be dealt with later.

Reference Chart

a A ant	b B bag	c C cat	d D dog	e E egg	f F fox
g G gum	h H hat	i I ink	j J jam	k K kiss	l L lemon
m M mat	n N nail	o O orange	p P pet	qu Qu quid	r R rat
s S sock	t T top	u U up	v V vet	w W wasp	y Y yes
z Z zebra	ch chip	sh ship	th then	th thin	ck lock

The vowel names

a / A as in ape	e / E as in even	i / I as in ice	o / O as in open	u / U as in unit	y / Y Later!

Coach

Ask your student to read out-loud, the **sounds** of the **consonants** and the sounds and **names** of the **vowels**, as you work down the **Pro** columns on the opposite page; ticking and dotting as appropriate.

Correct answers earn a tick; incorrect answers earn a dot.

Refer to the marking instructions on **pages 24 - 25** if you are unsure.

The **consonant sounds** are: **b** as in **b**ag **d** as in **d**og - **r** as in **r**at - **t** as in **t**ap **m** as in **m**at - **p** as in **p**et - **f** as in **f**ox etc. Vowel sounds are printed in green: a as in ant - e as in egg - i as in ink o as in orange - u as in up. Vowel names are printed in red: a as in ape e as in even - i as in ice - o as in open u as in unit. Students must know the difference between vowel sounds and vowel names **only**.

Consonant names must never be used!

When students encounter **vowels** in the columns opposite; they must say both sound and **name**. E.g. a sound a name - e sound e name i sound i name - o sound o name u sound u name.

The letter '**L**' has been written in both capitals and lower case letters (L - l) in order to avoid confusion with the letter 'i' (I).

Emphasize the use of the tongue when demonstrating '**th**' as in '**then**' or '**thin**'. The letters '**qu**' are always together in English: '**q**' on its own says '**c**'. Think of Ira**q**! Use the term 'kicking **k**' to describe '**k**'. Some students may have difficulty pronouncing the letters '**r**' and '**w**'. Many students find the letters '**b**' and '**d**' and also '**g**' and '**c**' confusing. Do not be dogmatic: If your student has problems with any of these letters (**b d g c**) you may correct your student without incurring a dot.

Do not attempt the same column twice in the same day: one attempt for one tick or dot!

Day							Day							Day							Day						
Month							**Month**							**Month**							**Month**						
Pro	kicking k *						Pro	tongue th *						Pro	together qu *						Pro	vibrate lips v *					
m							sh							p							d						
f							d							a a							v *						
h							w							g							th *						
a a							i i							z							u u						
l (L)							j							e e							l (L)						
b							th *							i i							c						
c							t							o o							s						
r							o o							n							ch						
k *							s							y							f						
y							p							b							t						
e e							u u							qu *							sh						
n							g							h							j						
ch							r							t							qu						

a sound **a** name	**e** sound **e** name	**i** sound **i** name	**o** sound **o** name	**u** sound **u** name

Coach

Spelling Basic Letter Sounds

You can be certain that your student is familiar with the sounds when he/she is able to spell them. Avoid letting your student see the columns. You must be able to monitor the spellings as they are written! Left-handed students are difficult to watch but you should be able to see if a word has been spelled correctly on the first attempt. **See seating - page 21.**

Note: Upper case (capitals) vowels are not entitled to say their **name** any more than lower case vowels!

Be prepared, once more, for the sound '**th**'. In these early stages you must emphasize the use of the tongue. The letters '**th**' can make two sounds: **hard** '**th**' as in '**th**en' and **soft** '**th**' as in '**th**in'. The **soft** '**th**' is often confused with the sound of the letter '**f**': **th**ree - **f**ree.
Use **hard** '**th**' to demonstrate the sound and explain **soft** '**th**' as and when it occurs in a proper word.

After placing the date in the date grid; work down the columns.

Ask your student to spell the letter sounds on the opposite page: '**a**' as in '**a**nt' or '**a**pple', '**b**' as in '**b**at' or '**b**ag', etc. **You must not say:** "**a**" as in '**a**corn' or "**b**" as in the word '**bee**' etc. You must say the letter sounds that have been used in the previous exercise.

Strategy

1) Coach reads a sound for student to spell.
2) Student must repeat the sound.
3) Student should then say the sound as he/she writes (spells) the sound.

Do not attempt the same column twice in the same day: one attempt for one tick or dot!

Follow the column guides. Speak clearly.

Day					Day					Day					Day				
Month					Month					Month					Month					
Spell	**Sounds only!**				Spell	**Sounds only!**				Spell	**Sounds only!**				Spell	**Beware ***				
a					*qu*					*n*					*d*					
b					*b*					*e*					*j*					
v					*h*					*v*					*qu*					
g					*o*					*z*					*th*					
l (L)					*j*					*y*					*a*					
f					*c*					*i*					*m*					
c					*k*					*o*					*l (L)*					
r					*s*					*u*					*r **					
ch					*w*					*h*					*w **					
t					*e*					*s*					*ch*					
y					*p*					*d*					*z*					
u					*i*					*sh*					*t*					
n					*m*					*w*					*sh*					
sh					*f*					*t*					*p*					
k					*th*					*ch*					*g*					

Important strategy: Spelling exercises require clear speech from coach and student. Make sure that your student is looking at your mouth when you speak. It is also vital that the student replies with each sound or word. Make sure you can see your student's mouth when he or she replies. The reply must come before attempting the spelling. **This strategy must become routine! *Some students may have difficulty pronouncing the letters 'r' and 'w'. Do not be dogmatic!**

Other Information

Many people with literacy problems have been taught the alphabet names and not the alphabet sounds (usually by well-intentioned parents or friends): a cardinal error! The name of the letter 'm' does not represent the sound 'em' as in '**em**blem' likewise the sound of the letter 'r' does not represent the sound 'ar' as in 'car'.

Coach

Basic Sounds

Column 1: Make sure you are familiar with these basic sounds which have been formed by sliding together the sounds learned on the previous page. Remember: Your student will spell that which he/she hears. Your student must know that this exercise is about constructing sounds. Pay attention to pronunciation. **Speak clearly!**

Column 3: The section highlighted in **column 3** is very important. Many students with weak spelling skills associate these sounds with the single consonant names alone: '**n s r f m l**'.

Watch carefully: If the letter '**m**' is written and then the '**e**' added to the front or just the letter '**m**' is written then a dot and not a tick has been earned. The sound '**ad**' has one '**d**'; make sure your student spells the **sound** '**ad**' and not the **word** '**add**'.

The sound '**ar**' says '**ar**' as in 'c**ar**'. If your student spells the word '**are**' then he/she is spelling from association with words and not building sounds. They have earned a definite dot!

Follow the column guides. Speak clearly.

Day Month Spell			Day Month Spell		Beware *	Day Month Spell		Beware *	Day Month Spell		Beware *
ib			eth *			en			ac		
ap			oth *			es			esh		
ol			ab			ar			af		
os			ub			ef			ec		
og			id			em			ic		
ig			et			el			oth *		
ug			ith *			ish			ud		
ep			ed			uch			eth *		
op			ush			ad			oc		
uf			un			osh			al		
um			om			ath *			il		
ag			eb			ob			ul		

Coach: **Beware: Emphasize the use of the tongue in these sounds.** *

Other Information

Modern attempts to ruin a student's grasp of the language allow avoidable symmetry to impede the flow and development of handwriting.

Good handwriting is not about flowery affectation but a means of organizing thoughts and speech on paper in a logical and sequential order.

The confusion between 'b' and 'd' becomes much less marked if the letters are not presented as an arbitrary choice between a ball to the left or right of a perpendicular line.

Some schools have banished the traditional letter forms and exercises and have thus helped to perpetuate the problem.

Coach

Consonant Vowel Consonant (CVC) Words

Ask your student to read the words on the opposite page by sliding the sounds together.

Column 4 Spelling
Speaking clearly is an instruction not an option!
When reading words for your student to spell you must:

1 Engage the student's attention.

2 Make sure you can see your student's mouth and that he/she can see yours.

3 When you have pronounced the word, your student must repeat it in order that you can mutually establish the correct word to be spelled.

This procedure must be adopted in the spelling exercises throughout the text.

Day						Day						Day						Day					
Month						Month						Month						Month					
Pro						Pro		Tongue *				Pro		Tongue *				Spell		Tongue *			
fen						hum						cod						*thin* *					
sap						lug						cog						*vat*					
mat						mob						fog						*rum*					
fig						mop						got						*sag*					
map						mid						hem						*that* *					
hip						sub						pig						*fat*					
nor						rig						vet						*dash*					
jig						man						nod						*sham*					
lob						sat						fed						*chin*					
tug						pad						bid						*thug* *					
jug						bath *						chug						*chap*					
hug						rat						then *						*mash*					
wit						beg						than *						*bid*					
rut						him						them *						*them* *					

Coach

Reading and Spelling Simple Words

This is a continuation of the previous exercise and it is important that we establish your student's ability to read and spell basic sounds before we introduce more complex sounds and rules.

The letter '**s**' has been added to the end of some words. This will have a greater impact later.

Follow the column guides. Speak clearly.

Day					Day					Day					Day				
Month					Month					Month					Month				
Pro					Pro					Pro					Spell				
quit					net					fan					path				
cob					cots					jars					shush				
tab					that					bush					ships				
gums					them					hen					shod				
bath					cash					char					jot				
quip					moths					ash					quit				
quid					cars					wish					shins				
sash					bash					hush					quip				
sham					sop					lush					posh				
moth					path					red					moth				
chub					shut					chats					quid				
shad					get					shot					fens				
chops					gad					shops					nibs				
chips					van					fin					rash				

Coach

Vowel Discrimination

**The object of the exercise:
Your student must know the difference
between** vowel sounds **and** vowel names!
It is crucial!

The **consonant names** are not used in English
but they do cause problems for learners.

**On no account must the student attempt to
read or write the full words for the coach.
Student must say and write the vowels alone!**

Column 1
The coach must say the word "**full**".
The student must select the **vowel sound** and
say: "**u sound**" and then write the letter 'u'.

The coach must say the word "**top**".
The student must select the **vowel sound** and
say: "**o sound**" and write the letter 'o'. Continue
working down the column.

Column 2
The coach must say the word "**cope**".
The student must select the **vowel name** and say:
"**o name**" and write the letter 'o'.
The coach must say the word "**tape**".
The student must select the **vowel name** and say:
"**a name**" and write the letter 'a'. Continue working
down the column.

Column 3
The coach must say the word "**gut**".
The student must select the **vowel sound** and say:
"**u sound**" and then write the letter 'u'.

The coach must say the word "**bone**".
The student must select the **vowel name** and say:
"**o name**" and write the letter 'o'.

The coach must say the word "**mile**".
The student must select the **vowel name** and say:
"**i name**" and write the letter 'i'. Continue
working down the column.

Day Month **Vowel Sounds**		Both correct to earn a tick!		Day Month **Vowel names**		Both correct to earn a tick!		Day Month **A mixture**			All three correct to earn a tick!			
full	top			cope	tape			gut	bone	mile				
keg	hiss			Pete	male			dene	tag	bide				
tin	rap			kite	hope			hake	leg	rake				
quit	yen			bide	fuse			dug	muse	chub				
hip	thug			pale	dome			vine	these	moss				
lag	jog			gape	mule			game	cute	push				
lab	pill			ripe	puke			pike	chase	hop				
nap	seg			ride	eke			gap	tame	mute				
dim	rob			gale	mole			miss	tome	wet				
log	fan			hide	bloke			ram	code	joke				
tell	mud			tide	theme			fen	file	kit				

Your student must not spell the whole word. Students must listen to the coach reading the word then select and spell the correct **vowel sound** or **vowel name** alone!
Example: **'a' as in 'ant'** or **'a' as in 'cape'**.

Other Information

The partial introduction of 'end blends' is needed in order to explain the use of the letter 'k'. The silent 'k' before an 'n' in words such as 'knee' and 'knock' will be dealt with later. In English the letter 'c' forms a 's' sound before 'i' 'e' or 'y' which will also be dealt with later.

Examples:

   cell cent cinder city cycle

Coach

Introducing the Rules for k and ck

The consonant 'k' and the combination 'ck' serve a particular purpose in our language. If a word ends with a **vowel sound** followed by 'c' **sound** we must use **ck**:

Examples: t**a**ck n**e**ck p**i**ck l**o**ck d**u**ck.

If a word ends with a **consonant sound** followed by a 'c' **sound** we must use '**k**'

Examples: sa**nk**, ma**sk**, bu**lk**, mi**lk** and pa**rk**

In English '**Kicking k**' alone forms a 'c' **sound** before 'i' or 'e'.

Examples: **ki**d **ki**t **ke**g **Ke**nt

From this point, green print will only be used to demonstrate the use of vowel sounds in new rules or as a reminder of rules learned previously.

Demonstrate the rules on scrap-paper before starting the exercise.

Follow the column guides. Speak clearly.

Day Month				Day Month				Day Month Spell				Day Month Spell			
Pro				Pro				*kit*				*shack*			
mo**ck**				k**i**p				*mock*				*suck*			
be**ck**				cat				*shock*				*lock*			
sho**ck**				K**e**n				*link*				*chick*			
ne**ck**				cut				*luck*				*bulk*			
pe**ck**s				k**i**d				*racks*				*lacks*			
la**ck**				can				*pock*				*check*			
tu**ck**				k**e**g				*milk*				*cash*			
wi**nk**				cub				*hank*				*pink*			
ta**sk**				k**i**t				*kick*				*hock*			
si**lk**				cop				*tuck*				*keg*			
pa**rk**				ki**nk**				*tack*				*thick*			
hu**lk**				cab											

Coach: Draw your student's attention to the rules as he/she works down the **Pro** columns. Example: (mo**ck**) **vowel sound 'o' use 'ck'** (be**ck**) **vowel sound 'e' use 'ck'** (combination **ck**) (wi**nk**) **consonant 'n' use 'k'** (ta**sk**) **consonant 's' use 'k'**. **K**ip and **K**en use 'k' before 'i' or 'e'.

Coach

Words Ending with Single or Double Consonants s - f - l

Column 1 Explain to your student that the words '**yes this bus plus gas**' are the only common words in English which end with a **vowel sound** and a single **consonant** '**s**'. All other words ending **vowel sound** followed by **consonant** '**s**' must have the final **consonant** '**s**' doubled.
Example: cr**oss** - f**uss** - conf**ess** - impr**ess**

Column 2 The same rule applies to words ending with a **vowel sound** followed by **consonant** '**f**'.
Example: g**aff** - sn**iff** - mast**iff** - midr**iff**. The word '**if**' breaks the rules.

Words like '**leaf**' and '**proof**' have vowels but not **vowel sounds**.

Column 3 The rule for double '**ll**' is more complex. The same rule applies to words ending with one **vowel sound** followed by '**l**'.
Example: f**ill** - sp**ell** - p**ull**. The rule breakers are '**nil**' and '**pal**'.

Words with more than **one vowel** need to end with just one '**l**'.
Example: disp**el** - comp**el** - fulf**il** - menth**ol**.

The basic **vowel sounds** are: '**a**' as in '**ant**', '**e**' as in '**egg**', '**i**' as in '**pig**', '**o**' as in '**dog**' and '**u**' as in '**gut**'. Bring this to your student's attention before attempting the columns.

Day				Day				Day				Day			
Month				Month				Month				Month			
Pro	exceptions *			Pro	exception - if			Pro	exceptions *			Spell			
mess				off				fill				*bell*			
boss				cuff				full				*doll*			
less				toff				pill				*impel*			
confess				quiff				consul				*until*			
unless				sheriff				mental				*miss*			
emboss				tariff				fulfil				*mass*			
obsess				handcuff				shall				*concuss*			
yes *				midriff				pull				*harass*			
this *				gaff				compel				*cuff*			
bus *				huff				dental				*quiff*			
plus *				puff				nil *				*pontiff*			
gas *				riff				pal *				*Cardiff*			

Coach: As your student reads down the **Pro** columns, draw his/her attention to the rules:
Vowel sound + double 'ss' 'mess' 'confess' exceptions: yes* this* bus* plus* gas*
Vowel sound + double 'ff' 'off' 'tariff' exception: if *
Vowel sound + (double 'll') 'fill' 'ill') exceptions: nil* pal* **more than one vowel** = (one 'l') 'fulfil' 'dispel'

Coach

Basic Spellings with the Addition of **S** and Final Double Consonants

If your student makes a mistake then he/she earns a dot. If you fail to analyse the reason why this has happened then you are treating the exercise as a spelling list.

This is not about memory! It is about using the rules of the language. Get out the scrap-paper and, where possible, demonstrate the error.

The Word Wasp has been designed to draw the coaches attention to weaknesses. Consistent dots reveal consistent errors. There will be a consistent reason! Work out why your student makes an error.

If students don't know the vowel sounds then they will not be able to distinguish between words that end in a vowel sound **followed by the letters s,f,or l. Your student must be able to explain why he/she has used a double or single consonant at the end of a word.**

Some words have an '**s**' added but the rules apply to the root word.

Make sure your student spells the root word correctly before adding the '**s**'.

examples: **root word:**   hill + s = hills
            root word: tiff + s = tiffs

You may inform your student that the words marked by the asterisks ($*$) are exceptions.

Follow the column guides.
Speak clearly.

Day Month Spell				Day Month Spell				Day Month Spell	exceptions *	Day Month Spell			
thick				tiff				yes *		Ross			
bells				naps				lack		lull			
pill				huffs				unless		lass			
gums				gaps				compel		cuff			
dull				buff				this *		plus *			
tins				bashful				mastiff		cartel			
shall				gaff				fans		quiff			
shell				fell				moss		rill			
sheds				off				fuss		hulks			
mull				tags				bus *		gas *			
logs				cuffs				jams		dispel			
yell				yen				fitful		nil *			
yank				riff				hiss		pal *			

Coach: Inform your student that the words 'us', 'is', 'as', 'his' and 'has' do not end with a 's' sound; they end with a 'z' sound. That is why they have only one 's'!

Coach

The Pronunciation Columns have Three Functions:

1 To illustrate a particular rule.
2 To hear the full pronunciation of words.
3 To tie spelling to speech.
When reading a word for your student to spell **you must pronounce every vowel sound.** In the word '**emblem**' we can only hear the first vowel: '**e**'. The second '**e**' is unstressed.

You must make sure that all vowels are stressed. It may not sound like the real word but your student will only spell that which he or she hears. The pronunciation columns and passages are for you to correct the pronunciation and tie spelling to speech.

'S' or 'es'?

The object of the '**Pro**' columns in this exercise is to show students that it is not always enough to form plurals by adding '**s**' alone. Sometimes we have to add '**es**'.

The rule is: If the word ends with the letter '**s**' (bu**s**), '**ss**' (lo**ss**), or '**sh**' (di**sh**) then the plural is formed by adding '**es**'.

Example: bu**ses** - lo**sses** - di**shes**

Note: The '**es**' plural is pronounced like the word '**is**'. The letter '**e**' regularly makes the sound '**i**' as in 'ink'.

Although we must speak for spelling there are occasions when we use other tactics: you may tell your student if he/she hears '**is**' at the end of a word; it is usually spelled '**es**'. Listen to the ending of the following words:

bu**ses** - mi**sses** - wi**shes**

If your student misses the double '**ss**' e.g. 'mi**s**es' instead of 'mi**ss**es'; remind your student to spell the root word first: spell '**miss**' then add '**es**'.

Day						Day						Day						Day					
Month						Month						Month						Month					
Pro	Both correct to earn a tick!			Pro	Both correct to earn a tick!			Spell				Spell			
hit hit**s**				dish dish**es**				*sacks*				*bushes*			
bit bit**s**				wish wish**es**				*pinks*				*masses*			
fan fan**s**				bush bush**es**				*links*				*hills*			
dig dig**s**				rush rush**es**				*kids*				*rashes*			
wit wit**s**				loss loss**es**				*larks*				*wishes*			
add add**s**				boss boss**es**				*bus* *				*toffs*			
rug rug**s**				pass pass**es**				*plus* *				*bosses*			
lid lid**s**				lass lass**es**				*forks*				*passes*			
fill fill**s**				fish fish**es**				*corks*				*buses* *			
bill bill**s**				bus bus**es**				*task*				*gases* *			
mill mill**s**				miss miss**es**				*nil* *				*pushes*			
tap tap**s**				kiss kiss**es**				*pal* *				*gushes*			

Coach: Inform your student that the words marked by the asterisks (∗) are exceptions.

Coach

The Letter n Before ch Says sh

The letters 'ch' make the sound 'sh' if they follow the letter 'n'. People who do not have literacy problems take this rule for granted. Listen to the sound of 'ch' in the word 'French'.

Example:

ranch sounds like ransh	bench sounds like bensh	pinch sounds like pinsh
conch sounds like consh	bunch sounds like bunsh	winch sounds like winsh

Your student must be able to explain that a 'n' before a 'ch' changes the sound to 'sh'. It is not enough for your student to remember individual words. The object of the Wasp programme is to teach your student the rules of English. We are not in the least interested in building a bank of regularly used words. As your student reads down the **Pro** columns, draw his/her attention to the rules.

The plural form of words ending in 'ch' observe the same rule as words ending 'ss' 's' or 'sh'.

E.g. bosses buses bushes lunches.

The rule is: 'n' before 'ch' makes it say 'sh'!

lunch = lunsh   lunches = lunshes

Follow the column guides. Speak clearly.

Day				Day				Day				Day			
Month				Month				Month				Month			
Pro				Pro				Pro				Spell	ch = sh after n		
lunch				picks				rasps				*quench*			
inch				inches				kin				*hunches*			
pinch				winches				Ken				*sashes*			
lulls				thank				benches				*link*			
rushes				tench				gasps				*lunches*			
fusses				sashes				ranks				*punches*			
cuffs				junk				kiss				*thinks*			
buses				ranches				tasks				*impel*			
punch				bench				keg				*shocks*			
gashes				hunches				lunches				*sharks*			
kisses				finches				kick				*pinches*			
finch				pinches				sharks				*Kevin*			

Coach: Spell the word **lunch** on scrap-paper both correctly and incorrectly: **lunch**, followed by: **lunsh**.

Read and Pronounce

Jack and the small lass called Jill had a hot red rash. Why was the well on the top of the hill?

A sick hack packs lunches with bunches of hot moss for the boss so nip to the shop and pick

the one that is not the Sun. Pinch off the tips and add a dash of milk to the dishes. Gaff then

stuff the char or shad with nuts and radishes. Put the shells on the shelf and fill in a chart to

fulfil the wishes of the man from the golf club. Lush is the bush that grows on the hills so sell

less of the dishes to the sheriff. Compel the man in the bushes to pass the lasses the dishes

that gave the consul the illness. Yes, this bus plus gas! Go to the back and pack! "How odd!"

said the men to have such a yen.   Add tar to a jar of jam and push a jack so far to the back

that the chuck compresses the lid. Fulfil the hard tasks and dispel the smell of the pig. Mush

the mesh and hush the fuss or you will miss the bus that runs on gas. Check the locks on the

shops and chat with a chum or shock the lad with a sack in the shack. Did Ken miss the lips

and kiss the kipper? Who will kiss a man who kisses kippers? "Not I", said the lass. "I will",

said the cat that ate the rat. Pinch less than an inch of the finches lunch.

Coach: Dates and dots are not required in this exercise or any following exercises which have the same two-box marking format. Mark a successful attempt with a tick; each tick required on a different day. You may assist your student with words in grey print.

Coach

Dictation

This exercise is vital in the development of a student's sequential processing skills.

Instruction

The coach must dictate a phrase or small sentence to the student. The student must repeat the phrase or sentence before writing it down. You may assist your student, where necessary, with capital letters and full stops.

Your student can ask you to repeat the phrase or small sentence before writing it down but once the writing process has started it must be completed, without assistance, to earn a tick.

If your student cannot complete the phrase or small sentence, or asks for assistance, then help and encouragement must be given. However, a dot has been earned! Do not leave a line unfinished.

Day								
Month								
Dictate								
Pick the radishes.								
A march can finish.								
had lunch with Jack								
Pinch the tench.								
Polish the benches.								
Finish the dishes.								
wishes for kisses								
Cut the losses.								
The tar is harsh.								
Marshes can vanish.								
March with a torch.								
silk on the cuffs								
not such bad lunches								

Coach

Final / End Blends

Columns 1 and 2: Your student must read both parts of each element correctly (**tan** followed by **tank**) to earn a tick. **Blends** are sounds made by two or more **consonants** which we mix together (blend) to form a single sound. To spell them correctly your student must be aware of the sounds/letters which form each blend.

Note: If your student cannot hear the last **consonants** of the words in these exercises; do not be surprised if he/she spells them incorrectly. Speak clearly and stress the last letters of each word. The sound '**n**' is particularly quiet in words like '**bend**', '**send**', '**fund**', etc.

Within some words, some sounds are very difficult to hear and your student may never have heard them before. The '**t**' on the end of words ending in '**ct**' (**See page 55)** such as 'se**ct**' and 'ta**ct**' are little more than soft clicks. **Make sure your student hears them!** The problem is more acute in words which end in complex end blends such as '**nct**' in a word like 'disti**nct**'.

Spelling: This is an exercise in **auditory discrimination** (listening to, and selecting sounds). It is a difficult exercise for many students. This exercise will sharpen your student's listening skills therefore it is important that you emphasize all the sounds. Be patient!

Follow the column guides. Speak clearly.

Day				Day				Day				Day				
Month				Month				Month				Month				
Pro				Pro				Spell				Spell				Beware *
tan tank				bon bond				*shelf*				*vend* *				
ban bank				fon fond				*jump*				*then* *				
lan land				far farm				*lamp*				*fend* *				
ben bend				char charm				*self*				*barks*				
len lend				lor lord				*charm*				*gulp*				
in ink				thin think				*think*				*help*				
dar dark				lef left				*thorn*				*month*				
nes nest				lif lift				*born*				*pulp*				
shar shark				pin pink				*thump*				*kiln*				
por pork				el elf				*shark*				*sunk*				
for form				sel self				*champ*				*shank*				
raf raft				lil lilt				*melt*				*tilt*				

Coach: **Beware:** The initial sounds (**v** **th** **f**) can be difficult to hear. Speak clearly! *

Day				Day				Day				Day			
Month				Month				Month				Month			
Pro				Pro				Spell				Spell			
end				fund				*barn*				*bulk*			
rend				tarn				*adorn*				*silk*			
tilth				quest				*attend*				*milk*			
tend				cost				*fork*				*hulk*			
filth				lost				*lark*				*sulk*			
land				fast				*mark*				*tilt*			
band				tart				*bump*				*wilt*			
ramp				rasp				*chimp*				*felt*			
sand				raft				*lump*				*bolt*			
hand				carp				*camp*				*wink*			
golf				harp				*damp*				*pink*			
pond				corn				*sump*				*port*			

Coach: **Bold letters** (double **consonants**): your student can be assisted without incurring a dot.

Day						Day						Day						Day					
Month						Month						Month						Month					
Spell	**Beware** *					Spell						Spell						Spell	**Say e not i or e** *				
ect						edict						attempt						intact					
ict						tact						depict						infect					
oct						duct						erupt						erect *					
uct						torpid						collect						bell					
opt						inept						contest						rebel					
ept						act						disrupt						effect *					
inct *						insect						corrupt						affect					
tect						defunct						reject						consent					
tinct						elect						induct						detect *					
funct						confess						attack						adopt					
unct						tempt						insect						facts					

Coach: The first column contains sounds not words. **Make sure your student is aware of this!** Make sure your student hears every letter in these complex end blends: especially '**c**' and '**t**'. Watch out for the words '**edict**' and '**contest**'. Students will hear '**edit**' and '**contess**'. Be aware of the words '**duct**' and '**tact**'. Your student may want to use the words '**ducked**' and '**tacked**'. The use of '**ed**' at the end of words will be explained later. Your student must only use the sounds learned previously. The student who spells the sound '**inct**' * by spelling the word '**inked**' or '**inkt**' is spelling by association and not from the sounds and rules learned earlier. **Discourage this practice now!**

Other Information

All variations of split syllables using both open and closed have been tried. The results have shown that some students hear some sounds better than others and the more students progressed the more discerning they became. Syllables with open ends (cv) were problematic with some students. Most students could hear the vowel sound 'i' at the end of an open syllable. Many students found the vowels 'a' and 'u' difficult to hear in the early exercises but the more they worked through the text the clearer the vowel sounds became. Splitting the words encourages coaches to stress the relevant vowel sounds, particularly in the final syllable, which tends to be left unstressed.

Coach

Divided Words

Some words will be divided in order to remind you to give your student clear sounds. Do not treat them as two words. Leave enough hesitation for the separate sounds to be heard clearly but pronounce them together as one word.

Note: This point will be stressed over and over again: **It is important that your student constructs the words from the sounds and rules they have learned without resorting to words which they might know already.**

Beware of the '**w**' which will be inserted after a '**q**' sound '**qw**'. Adults are particularly prone to **word association**. The earlier you stop this happening the easier your progress will be.

Follow the column guides. Speak clearly.

Day						Day						Day					
Month						Month						Month					
Spell						Spell	**Say e not i or e** *					Spell	**Say e not i or e** *				
quit						quilt						inches					
quid						quick						demand *					
quest						quiff						con tort					
li quid						request *						in sult					
equip						quack						var nish					
quench						ashes						tar nish					
quill						shush						self ish					
van quish						chunk						ad junct					
in quest						in vest						vic tim					
con quest						sashes						im pact					
con vict						un just						con duct					

Other Information

Received Sounds and Word Division

People with literacy problems, both children and adults, have usually muddled their way through to a level of literacy which is a product of received sounds; a familiarity with some essential words; sheer determination and guile.

I was first made aware of the problem of received sounds when it was pointed out to me that a dyslexic student under my tuition refused to order two breakfasts in a local cafe. It transpired that she couldn't say the word 'breakfasts'. The word she had always heard was 'breakfass' which meant that the plural was 'breakfasses'. She knew the word was wrong but was unable to contemplate an alternative. She had the same problem with many end blends which contained an 's'. She couldn't offer a plural to 'disk', 'fist' or 'mask'.

Coach

Difficult Sounds

Students will spell that which they hear: listen for the sound of the letter 't' in **fists** or the letter 'k' in **risks**. These barely audible sounds will be a problem for the coach who does not pronounce the words properly in the spelling columns that follow this exercise.

Strategy: Ask your student to spell the root word first.

Example: fist - fists   risk - risks

Follow the column guides. Speak clearly.

Day					Day					Day				
Month					**Month**					**Month**				
Pro	Both correct to earn a tick				**Pro**	Both correct to earn a tick				**Spell**	Both correct to earn a tick			
cask casks					shot shots					*tempt tempts*				
fist fists					rasp rasps					*gust gusts*				
risk risks					husk husks					*gasp gasps*				
lisp lisps					ask asks					*lisp lisps*				
last lasts					task tasks					*cask casks*				
mask masks					tusk tusks					*pest pests*				
rusk rusks					tempt tempts					*mask masks*				
rust rusts					fend fends					*fist fists*				
gust gusts					cusp cusps					*rust rusts*				
gasp gasps					kilt kilts					*pelt pelts*				
pond ponds					rot rots					*tent tents*				

Coach

Syllable Division / Word Analysis

Do not be afraid of the title! This is a simple exercise which will prepare your student for the spelling and reading of longer words. The exercise grid contains rows of words and sounds.

Ask your student to read an exercise row from left to right. When all five sections have been read correctly; you may tick the box.

Follow the column guides. Speak clearly.

Coach: Work from left to right. The five sounds or words must be pronounced correctly to earn a tick. Work from left to right - - - - - - - - - - - ->					Day Month															
>	an	van	nish	anish	vanish														
>	em	oss	bosses	emboss	embosses														
>	am	bush	ambush	bushes	ambushes														
>	in	kin	iskin	siskin	kinship														
>	on	con	fess	onfess	confesses														
>	ob	obs	ess	sess	obsesses														
>	in	inval	alid	valid	invalid														
>	ulp	pulp	pit	ulpit	pulpits														
>	in	fin	inish	finish	finishes														
>	ar	car	arpet	carp	carpets														
>	ick	thick	icket	thicket	pickets														
>	ack	pack	acket	packet	jackets														

Other Information

In English the letter 'e' often forms the sound we associate with the letter 'i'; particularly in a final syllable and particularly when followed by the letter 't'. Often, at the end of many words, with a few regional exceptions, 'et' sounds like 'it'.

Coach

Once More: e Can Say i

Your student may hear 'it' at the end of these words but they must be spelled with 'et'.

Example:

market
socket
packet

Although these words may sound as if the last vowel is making an 'i' **sound**; it is being spelled with the vowel 'e'; much the same as the rule for 'es': fusses dishes benches. Make your student aware of this before beginning the exercise.

Follow the column guides. Speak clearly.

Day					Day					Day					Day				
Month					Month					Month					Month				
Pro					Pro					Spell					Spell				
rock**et**					cult					*pocket*					*bill et*				
buck**et**					insult					*ticket*					*gask et*				
pock**et**					contact					*packet*					*con form*				
collect					lock**et**					*hal ibut*					*con sort*				
mark**et**					adult					*sen timent*					*con quest*				
limp**et**					sock**et**					*con duct*					*van quish*				
pull**et**					conject					*var nish*					*pick et*				
mall**et**					insist					*com pact*					*tarn ish*				
fill**et**					pick**et**					*res ident*					*admon ish*				
select					cask**et**					*sed iment*					*ob ject*				
thick**et**					invest					*con diment*					*jack et*				
contort					bask**et**					*car pets*					*con tact*				

Reminder: Two consecutive ticks are needed; each earned on a different day.

Other Information

There are exceptions to some rules but it is easier to learn these as such. Students with weak literacy skills see words as having their own individual shape and spelling. The sight of a small dictionary, which can have as many as 70,000 entries, must seem terrifying.

As part of the spelling programme, students are invited to look at the structure of words as they read and pronounce them. Students with spelling difficulties will often have reading difficulties; getting by as a result of reading familiar words and guessing others from the contextual evidence. Some students will be remarkably good at it!

Coach

Introducing the Rich Frame and the Silent t

In the first column, apart from those words highlighted, the 'ch' sound has a silent 't' before it. Most words ending with a 'ch' sound follow this rule:

If a word contains a vowel sound (not a vowel name) followed by a 'ch' then it requires a silent 't' between the vowel sound and the 'ch': catch pitch, unless the word can be found in the 'Rich* Frame' which contains words that break the rule.

The silent letter 't' and 'h' are highlighted in blue.

Your student must not pronounce the 't' but they must be aware of its presence in order to spell the words in the **Spell** columns. The plural form of words ending with a 'ch' 'sh' 's' 'ss' require 'es'.

ditches   dishes   buses   fusses

Ask your student why the words **porch**, **march**, **arch**, do not carry a silent 't'. The answer should be that such words do not end in vowel sound 'ch'.

Day		Day		Day		Day	
Month		Month		Month		Month	
Pro	Rule breakers *	Pro		Spell	Rule breakers *	Spell	
rich *		arches		*rich* *		*matches*	
such		match		*such*		*patches*	
much		catch		*much*		*larch*	
attach		torches		*attach*		*batches*	
detach		hutches		*detach*		*catches*	
which		parch		*which*		*march*	
ditch		Dutch		*pitch*		*fetches*	
pitch		larch		*vetch*		*hatch*	
patch		thatch		*hitch*		*torches*	
vetch		porch		*porch*		*pitches*	
hitch		ketch		*arch*		*ketch*	
notch		march		*patch*		*ketchup*	
latch		kitchen		*latch*		*thatch*	

Other Information

Initial Blends

Initial blends are notoriously difficult for some students to read or spell, particularly if the emphasis of their literacy education has been formed largely by word recognition techniques. This exercise begins to reveal the subtleties and range of phonetic expression and experience has taught us that the most effective way of teaching initial blends is to allow the student to spell initial blends before reading them.

There are schools of thought which prefer to use the actual sounds as they are formed in the words. The results tend to produce a battery of amorphous sounds often barely distinguishable from each other. By using the fully rounded sound, with the emphasis placed on the second consonant, the sound produced is more distinct and easier to recall.

Initial blends form a major plank in the phonic structure of many words. Once they have been learned, the door is open for more complex constructions.

Coach

Initial or Beginning Blends

Columns 1,2,3, and 4
Note: If you are unfamiliar with these sounds then get help before you start!

Initial blends:
These sounds are made by the blending/mixing of the two, and sometimes three, letters at the beginning of some words.

The coach must always make the distinction between sounds and words.

In the first two elements of **column 1**, the coach will ask the student to spell the sound '**br**' and tick or dot the box before asking the student to spell the word '**brim**'. Continue the exercise using the same method.

A note on emphasis:

The last letter of a blend should receive more emphasis than the first.

Day Month Spell					Day Month Spell					Day Month Spell					Day Month Spell				
br					fr					tw					str				
brim					frog					twin					strap				
bl					gl					sp					spr				
bled					glad					spot					sprat				
cl					gr					sm					scr				
clip					grip					smart					scrap				
cr					pl					sn					thr				
crop					plan					snap					thrust				
dr					pr					sw					shr				
drop					pram					swim					shred				
drag					prod					swill					shrub				
sl					tr					st					spl				
slack					trick					stack					split				

Other Information

This is not the place to introduce the soft 'c' rule. However, too many words would be missed if we left out the blends 'sc' and 'sk'.

There are exceptions to the rule: 'skate' and 'skunk'. Introducing these odd words would only serve to confuse.

Coach

Initial or Beginning Blends Continued

Columns 1 and 2: These columns show complex initial blends in action. Listen carefully to your student's pronunciation. They also show that we use the letter '**k**', not '**c**', before an '**i**' or an '**e**'. Be sure your student recognizes '**squ**' (**scw**) as in '**squid**'.

It is important for the coach to realize that the letters '**qu**' represent a blend of the letters '**c**' and '**w**'.

Columns 3 and 4: These are normal spelling columns.

Note: Unusual words: Thrips are well known amongst gardeners as garden pests. There will be many strange words for your student to spell but they are real words and will be used to extend your student's ability to use the mechanisms of our language.

The sounds and words in the **Pro** columns must be pronounced correctly to earn a tick.

Follow the column guides. Speak clearly.

Day					Day					Day					Day				
Month					Month					Month					Month					
Pro					Pro		k before 'e' & 'i'			Spell					Spell					
scr					skill					*brat*					*croft*					
shr					skin					*thrift*					*shift*					
squ					skid					*smug*					*twist*					
squid					skep					*scar*					*twill*					
spr					sk**etch**					*stretch*					*bless*					
str					skip					*skin*					*flesh*					
spl					scan					*splash*					*flash*					
thr					scamp					*clash*					*strand*					
sprint					sc**otch**					*grit*					*struck*					
thrips					scar					*grip*					*skill*					
split					scum					*glass*					*split*					
thrush					thrash					*crunch*					*shrink*					

Coach

More Initial or Beginning Blends

Once again: watch out for words like '**strict**'. If your student spells the word thus: '**stricked**', then you can be sure that he/she is not building from sounds.

'**Stricked**' is another example of spelling by association with words such as '**tricked**'. We will teach the sound made by the letters '**ed**' later.

If your student does not hear the letter sounds; do not be surprised if he/she does not spell them correctly. It's the coaches job to ensure that these sounds are heard.

Remind your student that longer words with more than one vowel require a single 'l' only: e.g.: handfu**l**.

Follow the column guides. Speak clearly.

Day					Day					Day					Day				
Month					Month					Month					Month				
Pro					Pro					Spell					Spell				
fluffs					abstract					*trend*					*im press*				
brushes					critical					*fluffs*					*com press*				
trench					ethical					*skilful*					*strict*				
trams					obstruct					*shrank*					*con strict*				
plug					medical					*squint*					*blushes*				
switch					ordinal					*crushes*					*ad junct*				
dram					cardinal					*crashes*					*district*				
sprigs					ligament					*fulfil*					*spell*				
shrift					conscript					*trunk*					*dispel*				
clinch					informal					*drift*					*planet*				
flinches					parchment					*inches*					*clashes*				
clench					ornament					*grasp*					*branch*				

Day					Day					Day					Day				
Month					Month					Month					Month				
Pro					Pro					Spell					Spell				
corn					emboss					*spec trum*					*med ical*				
pulp					Advent					*crit ical*					*eth ical*				
corm					adept					*prospect*					*ob struct*				
bulb					unjust					*re tract*					*ab stract*				
cult					embark					*stolid*					*or dinal*				
evict					elvish					*stretches*					*car dinal*				
glum					adrift					*predict*					*or nament*				
flank					scalpel					*con duct*					*parch ment*				
short					upheld					*instruct*					*in formal*				
shrill					inject					*respect*					*con script*				
splint					sprag					*shrap nel*					*lig ament*				

Coach: Students will not be familiar with many of these words. This exercise is designed to stimulate the transfer of sounds into spellings and not about expanding your student's vocabulary. It is a tough but a necessary exercise.

Day		Day		Day		Day	
Month		Month		Month		Month	
Pro	Tongue! *	Pro		Spell		Spell	Stress f and th *
import		clink		*squinch*		*in tegral*	
consent		crank		*publish*		*pess imist*	
indent		stark		*tilth*		*op tim ist*	
seventh *		induct		*deflect*		*pen tagon*	
respect		inlet		*establish*		*polit ical*	
enchant		intact		*plat form*		*publican*	
invest		pepsin		*dictum*		*elev enth*	
depend		perish		*nectar*		*twel f th* *	
respond		sacrist		*cul prit*		*wit ness*	
unless		revolt		*con form*		*sub script*	
method		habits		*en crust*		*invest ment*	
tranquil		inhabit		*resist*		*with stand*	
reflect		visits		*con duct*		*dem ocrat*	

Coach

Reading Simple Sentences

The sentences your student is about to read have been structured eccentrically in order to make it difficult to predict or guess words from a familiar context.

If each word in a line is read correctly then you may place a tick in the end box. Each line requires two ticks; each tick earned on a different day!

Reminder: Dates and dots are not required in this exercise or any following exercises which have the same two-box marking format.

Words in grey print

These words may conform to rules which have not yet been addressed. You can assist your student with these words. However, if you need to assist your student with one or more words in normal print; then you cannot tick the box.

Read and Pronounce

Pinch the last lunches from the benches at the match and get consent at Lent to inflict the district conflict on the lost cast and the black trench dogs. Friends often think that kinks in branches can make the brash thick when stuck in the back of a trash can. Lambast the crass thug and the man with the list that began with 'friend' and ended with 'bend' and was said to include words like button, shirt, have, and give, but no mention of the rules which move them. Skip to the rink and push a cart with skill. Embellish the mess with radishes or jam then do your best to impress and not distress a rich witch. A lost cardinal in pink lint can be sent to the West but a friend can orbit a bus with a smart cart from Dartford but not from Thatcham or Bath. Fetch and fletch the stick then stretch and scuff the string. Bend the ash across the bench to obstruct a notch with a stiff splint. Varnish a gift and send a friend to lunch on mutton chops and harness the trap to harass the man who lost the buttons on his jacket. A contract with the district witches instructs the prince to distract the black frog and casts a spell which sends the insects on a trip to thrash the thrips with brushes, held by thrushes from Yarm. Dispel the charms that harm the North and compel the singer to bring the songs that belong to a throng of friends from Kent.

Coach

Difficult Sounds

The '**ng**' word endings are difficult to hear. Taking your student through these words will help him/her realise the proper spellings when he/she encounters them in the spelling columns on the pages following this exercise.

You must hear the '**d**' in 'ami**d**st'. If you hear 'lenth' and not 'len**g**th' then a dot has been earned.

Many people will find these words both difficult to hear and say. Be patient.

Note:

The exercise will be counter-productive if the end product is anxiety.

Day	Day	Day	Day	
Month	Month	Month	Month	
Pro	Pro	Pro	Pro	**tongue th ***
in ing	un ung	on ong	an ang	
distant	run rung	ami**d** st	ran rang	
thing	h**atch**	song	clang	
wing	flung	cr**ut**ch	sang	
deposit	refresh	belong	leng len**g**th *	
sling	slang	clench	stren**g**th *	
scrimp	brings	throng	st**it**ch	
cling	bun bung	abrupt	gangs	
impact	support	among	slings	
string	stung	things	longs	
bring	clung	along	king	
sting	lungs	gongs	bringing	

Coach

Words with a Greek / Latin Root

Students have learned that words ending with a **vowel sound** followed by a '**c**' sound require the combination '**ck**' (ba**ck**). However, there are some exceptions: words from the Greek or Latin languages require a single '**c**' alone (man**ic**). Your student should be informed of the origin of these words when they meet them.

If possible, encourage your student to use a '**b**' with a tail (left). This will help them to make the distinction between '**b**' and '**d**'. It also provides a useful ascender.

When writing the '**b**' ask your student to start with the tip of the tail and move the pencil to the point where it meets the down stroke and then down and up then round in one continuous movement.

Day					Day					Day					Day				
Month					Month					Month					Month				
Spell					Spell					Spell					Pro		Greek *		
thing					*thong*					*slang*					thinking				
vending					*patches*					*clang*					strong				
sing					*sibling*					*bang*					mustang				
gulf					*stretches*					*clung*					fling				
string					*throng*					*gang*					hustings				
sketch					*scratches*					*length*					brandling				
bring					*oblong*					*flung*					ethnic *				
crunch					*prong*					*strength*					public *				
ringing					*belonging*					*stings*					cosmic *				
stench					*oviduct*					*lungs*					Catholic *				
singing					*gong*					*fangs*					frantic *				
stinging					*clinging*					*filth*					gastric *				

Coach: If you say 'lenth' and 'strenth' instead of 'len**g**th' and 'stren**g**th' then you cannot expect your student to give you the correct spelling!   Remind your student of the Greek origins.*

Day						Day					Day						
Month						**Month**					**Month**						
Pro						Spell		**Greek** *			Spell						
fangs						*ab sorb*					*hospital*						
str**eng**th						*ethnic* *					*demolish*						
am**ong**						*gas kets*					*blem ish*						
am**ong**st						*mus kets*					*adrift*						
len**g**th						*defunct*					*sporting*						
str**eng**then						*shar pen*					*su**pp**ort*						
s**ing ing**						*report*					*abrupt*						
longest						*abscond*					*splashes*						
lungs						*smelting*					*defending*						
ami**d**st						*in stinct*					*susp ect*						
conquest						*organic* *					*aspects*						
antics						*depict*					*pro spect*						

Coach: As you might expect, words will become longer as you work through the text. Spelling requires the same constructional skills to build words from sounds as it does to read them. The Word Wasp exploits this fact which is why it is vastly superior to those schemes which suppose otherwise. Do not allow your students to guess. **The rule is: Build or Bust!**

Coach: Find - mark - and pronounce! Your student must find the vowel and make the correct vowel sound: a as in apple, e as in egg, i as in ink, o as in odd, u as in up, then place a tick in the box underneath it.

c	a	d	c	e	f	p	v	i	p	c	b	o	n	c	u	p	c	i	t	c	u	w	c	x	a

Coach: Find - mark - and pronounce! The vowels below are now printed in red. Ask your student to find and pronounce them. This time the vowels must say their **name**. Their **names** are: a as in ape, e as in even, o as in over, i as in island and u as in union. Your student must find the vowel; say its **name**; then place a tick in the box underneath it.

r	i	d	c	a	i	r	c	f	e	c	a	t	p	c	u	e	c	o	c	a	g	a	c	i	o

Coach: Find - mark - and pronounce! Ask your student to find and pronounce the sound of the green vowels and the name of the red vowels. Tick the box underneath the correctly pronounced vowel. There are 21 vowels in this exercise of which 9 say their **name** and 12 say their sound.

f	r	i	t	p	e	o	f	u	m	o	m	i	v	a	k	r	a	t	a	n	o	w	d	a	m

u	h	j	o	e	t	p	u	c	k	g	i	o	f	b	m	h	g	a	p	i	p	z	f	u	a

Coach

Mute - Silent or Magic e

The power of the vowel usually moves from right to left.

If we add the letter '**e**' to the end of the word '**l**o**p**' we form a new word: '**l**o**pe**'.
The '**e**' stays **silent** or **mute**. However, the vowel is still active. Vowels, particularly the letter '**e**', have the power to influence the sound of other letters, particularly other vowels. In this case the '**e**' can be described as firing its power through the '**p**' and into the vowel '**o**' which makes it say its **name**. Its **name** is '**o**' as in 'b**o**ne'.

The **Pro** column invites the student to read each line of letters, sounds and words. The vowels which have received the power of the **silent** '**e**' are now shown in **red** print and therefore must say their **name**.

Don't forget: the '**e**' at the end remains **silent** and from now on **silent** letters, for demonstration purposes, will be printed in **blue**.

Note: In the first spelling column the order of the words has been switched at random in order to prevent students from guessing.

Day				Day				Day			
Month				Month				Month			
Pro	**All correct to earn a tick**			Spell	**Both correct to earn a tick**			Spell			
a a al ale gale				*mat mate*				*convene*			
e e es ese these				*cope cop*				*these*			
i i ip ipe pipe				*tape tap*				*smiles*			
o o om ome dome				*cute cuts*				*dale*			
u u ute cute				*pine pins*				*stale*			
				dime dim				*stole*			
slime rose prose				*lop lope*				*clone*			
bone stripe strike				*fad fades*				*zone*			
compete impede				*tripe trip*				*bone*			
stampede complete				*use us*				*fuses*			
delete condone				*grip gripe*				*confuse*			
mundane insane				*rip ripe*				*infuse*			

Day						Day						Day						Day					
Month						Month						Month						Month					
Pro						Pro						Spell						Spell					
dim						vast						*note*						*distract*					
dime						note						*gulch*						*strand*					
drive						jibe						*trend*						*puke*					
grove						spade						*vale*						*vole*					
shift						tope						*shrike*						*divide*					
shale						sole						*lane*						*bane*					
stale						pike						*pike*						*bone*					
froth						larch						*strove*						*alone*					
graft						hake						*strive*						*Mike*					
theme						slime						*thrive*						*Steve*					
smoke						halibut						*cove*						*junk*					
drone						crave						*clench*						*im pute*					

Day						Day						Day						Day					
Month						Month						Month						Month					
Pro						Pro						Spell						Spell					
skint						prime						*flame*						*glide*					
dismal						slim						*cannot*						*im pede*					
diminish						blade						*prank*						*stam pede*					
flapjack						weld						*fund*						*com pete*					
banquet						crave						*funds*						*com plete*					
mode						flitch						*sends*						*invite*					
ingrate						throne						*bribe*						*chime*					
cataract						grape						*crank*						*close*					
depict						held						*broke*						*en close*					
matchless						shave						*arrive*						*dis close*					
harlequin						like						*adrift*						*in cline*					
trenchant						slave						*jibe*						*ad here*					

Coach

More Mute e and the Trigraph ire

The **Pro** column on the opposite page introduces the sound 'ire' as in 'tire'. It obeys the mute 'e' rule but the letter 'r' is difficult to hear.

Before you begin the exercise, write the word/sound 'ire' on scrap-paper and show your student how the addition of the 't' makes the word 'tire' and 'h' makes the word 'hire'.

Introducing Key Sounds or Words:

Key Sounds or **Key Words** will be noted by the letters **KS** or **KW** against the appropriate element.

Note: To avoid the following spellings: **ier / eir** remind your student that the 'ire' endings must finish with the **mute** 'e'

Follow the column guides. Speak clearly.

Day				Day				Day				Day			
Month				Month				Month				Month			
Pro	Key Word *			Pro				Spell				Spell			
ire KW *				define				*desire*				*shire*			
fire				probe				*conspire*				*lavish*			
desire				affect				*inspire*				*divine*			
spire				scribe				*aspire*				*effect*			
habit				entire				*compose*				*predict*			
tire				compel				*compute*				*polite*			
retire				scrimp				*condone*				*require*			
inspire				shrimp				*quake*				*spring*			
require				acquire				*trombone*				*squire*			
suppose				effect				*scorching*				*refute*			
admire				empire				*until*				*suspect*			
ozone				trade				*lem on ade*				*ozone*			

Coach: The 'ire' ending obeys the **mute** 'e' rule but makes one complete sound. Ask your student to spell 'ire' as in 'tire'!

Coach

More Mute e - the ore Trigraph

Before you begin the exercise, write the word '**ore**' on scrap paper and show your student how the addition of '**s**' makes the word '**sore**' and '**m**' makes the word '**more**'.

Don't forget: Never attempt the same column more than once in the same day!

Follow the column guides. Speak clearly.

Day				Day				Day				Day			
Month				Month				Month				Month			
Pro	**Key Word** *			Pro				Spell				Spell			
ore KW *				before				*more*				*con fine*			
more				combine				*store*				*in vade*			
store				drive				*before*				*deplore*			
core				contrive				*im plore*				*hire*			
tore				tome				*standing*				*occult*			
snore				until				*quest*				*flunk*			
save				score				*restores*				*brash*			
saves				convene				*thrives*				*respire*			
adores				votes				*cones*				*shore*			
sprite				gore				*clone*				*gore*			
sprites				restore				*clones*				*ignore*			
spore				estate				*decline*				*snore*			

Other Information

Repeated words have been deliberately duplicated because they have shown to be problematic. The word 'strength' is such a word.

Our apologies to students and coaches from the North East, and other regions for whom the 'ure' sound does reflect the mute 'e' rule.

Coach

The Trigraph **ure**

The Trigraph '**ure**' shares the same structure as both the **ire** and **ore** trigraphs but the vowel '**u**' **does not** say its **name**! The Trigraph '**ure**' sounds like the word '**your**'. The '**ure**' doesn't cause a problem in words such as 'c**ure**', 'p**ure**' and 'manic**ure**'. It is only when a '**t**' comes before '**ure**' that students have difficulty.

Example: pic**ture** struc**ture** den**ture**

The '**t**' before '**ure**' almost sounds like a '**ch**'. Ask your student to use a '**t**' before '**ure**' and not a '**ch**'.

For those students who fail to grasp the concept above; you will have to revert to **speaking for spelling** and form the '**t**' sound.

Example: pic**t ure**   struc**t ure**   den**t ure**
Correct the pronunciation in the **pro** columns.

All Three Trigraphs end with '**silent e**' (**ire - ore - ure**).

Follow the column guides. Speak clearly.

Day								Day									Day							
Month								Month									Month							
Pro	Key Sound *							Spell									Spell							
ure KS *								vulture									rid icule							
cure								culture									man icure							
pure								picture									armature							
manure								dispute									still							
secure								tribute									pestil							
stagnate								strength									ped icure							
denture								con trite									demure							
magnate								confess									procure							
adult								stature									an imate							
vulture								suspire									spitfire							
obscure								denture									congress							
longing								spore									indenture							

Hornet Students

From this exercise on, Hornet students will be required to earn two consecutive ticks before each element of an exercise can be considered as complete.

Please refer to the exercise instructions on pages 24 to 25 if you need further guidance.

Coach

The Two Names of U

Your student must understand that the letter 'u' has two **names**:

1) 'u' as in '**cube**' or '**cute**' sounds the same as '**you**'.

2) 'u' as in '**flute**' or '**true**' sounds the same as '**who**'.

Note: In many words the '**t**' before '**u**' can sound like a '**ch**'. Ask your student to use a '**t**' before '**u**' and not a '**ch**' examples: **t**ube - institute. Make sure that you pronounce the word '**d**une' with a '**d**'. It is easy to form a '**j**' in front of the 'u' which will produce the wrong sound for spelling.

Many students will be tempted to insert the '**you**' (ch**you**b). This is because they associate the sound 'u' with the word '**you**': be ready to correct them!

Follow the column guides. Speak clearly.

Day							Day							Day						
Month							Month							Month						
Pro							Spell							Spell						
mute							*flute*							*substitute*						
cute							*plume*							*ridicule*						
duke							*lute*							*solitude*						
tube							*prune*							*destitute*						
fuse							*untrue*							*confuse*						
abuse							*prude*							*attitude*						
rude							*bemuse*							*institute*						
prude							*amuse*							**imm**une						
brute							*cube*							*constitute*						
Luke							**d**une							*accuse*						
rule							**d**unes							*consume*						

Coach

Read and Pronounce Revision

This is another 'Read and Pronounce' sentence grid. Tick the box for each successful attempt. **Dots and dates are not necessary**. Each line has to be read twice successfully but never attempt the same line twice on the same day.

Words in grey print:

These words may conform to rules which have not yet been addressed. You can assist your student with these words. However, if you need to assist your student with one or more words in normal print then you **cannot** tick the box.

Students, having reached this exercise, are just as capable of breaking down words into their sounds and rules as they are capable of building them. They are not always aware of this. It is your job to show them!

Read and Pronounce

Push the cube in the tube and send it as a tribute in gratitude to the hungry multitude.

Cure the illness by drinking plenty of liquids and go to the store for some more red pills.

Defy the vulture and hang up a picture and if in dispute be resolute and play the flute.

In the event of bones being bent; take a pinch of snuff and some fresh liniment and rub

them with relish but do not venture to use the same hands to clean your dentures

because if you do they might set like glue but you will be sure that your teeth will be

secure. Strive at length to regain strength and take some time or you may decline.

Rotten flesh is fine for a vulture, they have no teeth just hard gums which they often

use when they consume plums or prunes. I have not the desire to restore the fire.

You may venture in the park when it's wet or when it's dark because ghosts there are

not, but my instinct thinks that a distinct mole is often the sole dark mammal in a hole.

Take note of the blokes that sing out of tune and ignore the bells that ring in the dales.

Other Information

Here, There and Where.

Our grandfathers would have had little difficulty with the following words: 'there' and 'where'. Both words rhymed with 'here' and in some parts of Yorkshire they still do. However, it is not the rhyme but the spelling which can be linked. Each word is about a geographical location and each word contains the word 'here': **here**, t**here**, w**here**.

The word 'here' follows the mute 'e' rule and silent 'h' has also been introduced so this is the appropriate place to introduce these words and they will be repeated together again and again.

The silent 'h' in many words was once spoken. However, it came at the beginning of the word and was an invitation to aspirate before the 'w'. In deference to history, (and to confuse further generations) the 'h' has been moved to follow the 'w' but the former pronunciation has been dropped.

Coach

Here There Where and Silent h

Column 1 introduces a silent letter: 'h'. The rule is that 'h' is silent after a 'w'.

Column 2 introduces the words '**here**', 'w**here**' and 't**here**'. The word '**here**' follows the **mute 'e'** rule which we have been dealing with over the last few exercises. Point out to your student that all these words are concerned with places and contain the word '**here**' and '**here**' is a place.

'W**here**' is a place (some w**here**, anyw**here**, w**here** it happened).

Here is a place. T**here** is a place. W**here** is the place?

To spell these words correctly, the student must make sure that each contains the **Key Word** '**here**' which also informs your student that the words are all about places.

Column 3 contains **mute 'e'** plurals.

Day					Day					Day					Day				
Month					Month					Month					Month				
Pro	**Silent h**				Pro	**KW key word** *				Spell					Spell				
wh**i**st					scrip**ture**					*whim*					*brisk*				
wh**a**le					Japanese					*whelp*					*struck*				
f**uture**					anthem					*arches*					*mental*				
wh**i**te					quintet					*scale*					*compel*				
wh**i**le					requ**ire**					*gales*					*emboss*				
wh**e**n					wh**e**lk					*which*					*whisk*				
wh**i**ch					grebe					*infect*					*scalpel*				
wh**i**p					glebe					*moles*					*distress*				
rapt**ure**					mere					*voles*					*sketch*				
wh**i**sk					**here** KW *					*here*					*conch*				
brine					t**here**					*there*					*skiff*				
wh**i**ff					w**here**					*where*					*mastiff*				

Coach

ism and asm and Redundant Vowels

Some of the words in the spelling columns contain the 'sm' final blend. These tend to be medical or scientific terms.

Explain that the end blend, notably 's' before an 'm', makes a 'z' sound and with the vowel 'i', the overall sound is 'izm'. The 'a' with the 'sm' final blend makes the sound 'azm':

Page 100 Read and Pronounce: With the exception of words in grey print, your student must read every word in a line correctly to earn a tick.

The word '**ghost**' (**Page 100**) is particularly important for The Word Wasp and the letters highlighted in red will reappear later.

Northern coaches only: (Page 101) You may have difficulty with the words '**some**', '**become**' etc. For spelling purposes, they should share the same vowel sound 'o' as in '**dog**'.

Follow the column guides. Speak clearly.

Day			Day			Day			Day		
Month			Month			Month			Month		
Pro			Spell			Spell			Pro		
bapt**ism**			*antag onism*			*shank*			core		
atav**ism**			*sarc asm*			*thrift*			deplore		
activ**ism**			*pess imism*			*console*			store		
solips**ism**			*cat abolism*			*adore*			require		
Budd**hism**			*organ ism*			*score*			before		
optim**ism**			*endo plasm*			*picture*			while		
conform**ism**			*embol ism*			*culture*			which		
sp**asm**			*Calvin ism*			*endure*			**here**		
sarc**asm**			*astig matism*			*more*			**there**		
catapl**asm**			*capital ism*			*sore*			**where**		
ectopl**asm**			*metab olism*			*tore*			white		
sarcopl**asm**			*method ism*			*pending*			whisk		

Coach: i**sm** = i**zm**   a**sm** = a**zm**

Read and Pro: Introducing ee

Double ee: The first 'e' says its **name** 'e' and the second 'e' is silent but activates the **name** of the first 'e'. Enigmatic plastic pants are often seen on the bottoms of bees. They stop them from stinging men but not so chimpanzees. Ethel Stritch from West Shoreditch did not like her classmates. She left her school and all its rules for a distant landscape. There she sits quite free of zits, applying lots of lipstick to her lips and other bits, while eating lemon pancakes.

Coach: Ask your student to take note: The silent 'e' has no power in the words are, none, gone, done, some, one, or become. Remind your student to use 'ee' where necessary on **Page 101**.

It went from **here** to t**here**. Has she g**o**ne? Did it c**o**me? It will take s**o**me time!

Some went t**here**. She has d**o**ne it. The buses ar**e** **there**. Are the jobs d**o**ne?

Words about places such as t**here** and w**here** contain the word **here**.

Question: Are t**here** such things as ghosts?

Answer: Only the ghosts that haunt some words!

Reminder: You may assist with words in grey letters. Dates and dots are not required.

Day			Day			Day			Day		
Month			Month			Month			Month		
Pro	silent e has no power *		Pro			Spell			Spell		
one *			income *			bee			cute		
done			welcome *			agree			amuse		
gone			pedigree			agreed			abuse		
none			spleen			destitute			secure		
shone			breed			degree			while		
some *			free			tree			conflict		
come			three			fortitude			shrine		
become			here			emigrate			one *		
are			there			freedom			done		
tree			where			some *			gone		
preen			speech			come			none		
ghost			freedom			become			shone		

Coach: In this exercise the five words or sounds must be pronounced correctly to earn a tick. Work from left to right: - - - - - - - - - - - - ->				Day Month									
>	ant	tant	antrum	tantrum	trumpets							
>	inch	pinch	inchpin	linchpin	clinches							
>	desp	atches	patches	despatch	despatches							
>	etch	tetch	tretch	stretch	stretches							
>	cult	agricul	ulture	culture	agriculture							
>	ist	dist	tress	stress	distressing							
>	and	hand	icap	dicap	handicap							
>	een	teen	eenth	teenth	fifteenth							
>	sag	sagree	disag	disagree	agreement							
>	esp	resp	espon	respon	responding							
>	apar	part	apart	artment	apartments							
>	orm	form	inform	deform	conforming							
>	arm	farm	charm	armless	charmless							

Read and Pronounce

Drench the French artist in the dock. Swim or sprint to the plinth and squint at the tench as it strums

a tune with attitude. Promote the dugong along with the dude. The white paragon from Kent must

admonish the reptile from Teesdale but only if it invigorates the blue free radicals from the State of

Tennessee. Prisms bend light and spasms bend muscles. Moby Dick was a white whale. When

whelks and crabs are fresh do not whack them with a stick or dump them whole in bottomless pits.

Crocodiles kept in small tanks will soon overwhelm your goldfish and bite the hand that feeds them,

so respect a crocodile kept in a kitchen. A vampire bat or a green mamba can upset a vulture.

While playing whist do not risk showing your hand to the man in the white hat with the greenish tint

if he squints. Cultivate organic carrots but do not panic if the hedonism of the absentees makes the

barbarism within the garden seem like a prospect for the future. Until the tuba from Cuba dispels the

white worms from the historic orchard, the King and Queen will only consume prunes, plums, blue

damsons, fresh figs, flatfish, crabs, pollack, haddock and dates on weekends in June.

Other Information

The predominance of the Roman angular script over the rounded Celtic form led to recognition problems. The mute 'e' on the end of words which ended with the sound 'v' was a way of distinguishing between the letters 'v' and 'u'.
Many years ago these letters were interchangeable. The 'e' announced that the last letter of a word was a 'v' and not a 'u'.

Coach

English Words Cannot End in the Letter V

The letter 'v' cannot form the end of words in English: we must always add a **silent** 'e'. Explain this to your student.

A note for northern coaches only:

When the words '**glove**', '**love**', '**shove**', etc., find their way into the spelling columns you should pronounce the letter 'o' as the 'o' in '**dog**'. '**Luv**' might be closer to your accent or that of your pupil and it is perfectly acceptable as part of his/her speech but your student needs to hear the sound 'o' in order to spell the word. The authors too, have northern accents and appreciate the problem.

Note: You may need to help your student with the words '**prove**', '**move**' and '**improve**'. They rhyme with each other which should make your task easier.

Follow the column guides. Speak clearly.

Day	Day	Day	Day
Month	Month	Month	Month
Pro	Pro	Spell	Spell
love	give	*pensive*	*venue*
above	valve	*expensive*	*im bue*
glove	shelve	*conscript*	*clue*
dove	active	*scripture*	*blue*
shove	involve	*have*	*true*
solve	delve	*one*	*presume*
have	imbue	*done*	*con strue*
move	blue	*gone*	*love*
remove	due	*none*	*above*
prove	glue	*here*	*glove*
improve	sue	*where*	*dove*
approve	untrue	*there*	*shove*

Day						Day						Day						Day					
Month						Month						Month						Month					
Pro						Pro						Pro						Spell					
indicate						give						repent						*object*					
absorb						forgive						redeem						*objective*					
elasticate						estate						crampon						*undue*					
dedicate						needful						flinching						*instinct*					
brandish						blemish						hatchet						*instinctive*					
avenue						ornate						massive						*captive*					
revenue						requite						stress						*vampire*					
retinue						one						stresses						*move*					
chicken						done						dress						*remove*					
continue						crash						dresses						*prove*					
require						crashes						feminism						*improve*					
morbid						travel						torment						*approve*					

Day					Day					Day					Day				
Month					Month					Month					Month					
Pro					Pro					Pro					Spell	**silent h ***				
commute					inculcate					subject					*sublime*					
mundane					compuls**ive**					unt**il**					*absentee*					
frac**ture**					informat**ive**					pass**ive**					*depress*					
impl**ore**					economist					mor**ass**					*anagram*					
transp**ire**					investigate					sk**etch**ing					*magnetism*					
inform					transmute					import					*culminate*					
struc**ture**					transpose					innings					*eliminate*					
retinue					transport					illustrate					*galvanism*					
impuls**ive**					object**ive**					subdue					*dogmatism*					
fustigate					endure					glob ule					*w**h**ite* *					
transmit					cap**ture**					fulf**il**					*w**h**eel* *					
engrave					subsume					dandr**uff**					*w**h**ack* *					

Coach

Losing the Silent e and Twin Consonants

All vowels have the power to make other vowels say their **name**. If we remove the **mute** 'e' from the root word '**smile**' and add '**ing**' then the 'i' in 'ing' will have the same effect as the mute 'e': **smiling**.

A vowel separated by just one **consonant** from another vowel is often made to say its **name**. '**Ridding**' becomes '**riding**' because the removal of one letter (**d**) allows the vowel 'i' in 'ing' to affect the vowel 'i' in 'riding'.

'Filing' becomes 'filling' because the extra **consonant** forms a double barrier and thus protects one vowel from the power of the other!

Two consonants block the power of the vowels. There are exceptions but not many!

Spelling:

Work from left to right, reading the spellings one word at a time. Give your student time to complete each spelling before moving to the next.

Ask your student to spell all the words in a row not a column. Every word in one row must be spelled correctly to earn a tick.

Two ticks earned on different days are needed to complete each row.

This exercise does not require dates or dots. Mark a successful attempt with a tick.

All the words in a row must be **pronounced** correctly to earn a tick.			All the words in a row must be **spelled** correctly to earn a tick.		
Pro			**Spell**		
file files filing filling			*slop slope sloping slopping slopes*		
drive drives driving			*hop hopping hope hoping*		
bake bakes baking			*bide biding bid bidding bides*		
make maker making			*pin pine pines pinning pining*		
dive dives diving			*slid slides sliding riding ridding*		
tap tapping tape taping			*cope cop coping doping mopping*		
include includes including			*slim slime slimming trimming*		
invade invades invading			*win winning wine wines*		
escape escapes escaping			*din dine dines dining dinner*		
hope hoping hop hopping			*quote quotes quoting*		
scrap scrapping scrape scraping			*shades wades wading shading*		
kit kite kitten kites			*cut cute cutting mute mutes lutes*		
cope coping scopes copes			*fuss fuse fussing fusing fuses infuse*		
rob robe robbing robes			*lop lope loping lopping topping ropes*		

Twin letters (consonants) stop the power of the vowel.

Coach

The Three Uses of y

Listen to the 'y' in the following words:

'y' saying 'y' as in 'yes' or 'beyond'.

'y' saying 'i' as in 'fly' or 'nylon'.

'y' saying 'i' as in 'happy' or 'system'.

Demonstrate the three uses of 'y' above to your student.

You can inform your student that the letter 'y' often acts as a vowel! It never says 'why'!!

Follow the column guides. Speak clearly.

Day		Day		Day	
Month		Month		Month	
Pro		Pro		Pro	
yardarm		ver**y**		dignif**y**	
nast**y**		def**y**		**s**ystem	
rectif**y**		den**y**		clar**i**fy	
n**y**lon		dust**y**		m**y**th	
Ban**y**an		cheek**y**		st**y**lus	
sk**y**lark		p**y**lon		**yo**del	
storm**y**		simplif**y**		hol**y**	
h**y**brid		edif**y**		holl**y**	
s**y**llabub		satisf**y**		compl**y**	
be**y**ond		solidif**y**		frost**y**	
s**y**mbol		froth**y**		appl**y**	

Coach: **y** saying **y** (as in **y**es) - **y** saying **i** (as in ver**y**) - **y** saying **i** (as in fl**y**)

Day					Day					Day				
Month					Month					Month				
Spell	y says y as in yes				Spell	y says i as in very				Spell	y says i as in fly			
yelps					sympathy					try				
yelling					party					deny				
York					funky					defy				
yapping					crunchy					spry				
canyon					twenty					my				
yardstick					symbol					myself				
beyond					seventy					rectify				
yomping					crispy					imply				
yank					risky					magnify				
yelping					Sycamore					modify				
yarn					husky					sky				
yippee					chunky					type				

Coach: As 'y' acts as an 'i' then we need to use 'k' to form a 'c' sound before it! (sky risky)

Read and Pronounce

Introducing the short cut X

Reminder: Dates and dots are not required.

The girl above gave the glove a shove and it fell from above. Mix the sticks and send a fax to the man from Halifax. Take a missive to the woman at the exit and expedite a reply but try not to terrify the bride inside as she hides from the man from the Inland Revenue who came along the avenue on his bike. Strike it from the records and compel a bloke to indicate where his wife will feed should he strive to have lunch by a stretch of land by the shore. If he should shove the shovel for his living he will have sore hands and picture the structure and the mixture of fixtures hanging from a stand in the kitchen. This means nothing to a vulture. It has habits from a distant culture. "Are you sure that this melon is mature?" asked the Empress. Explore stores, ignore carnivores and adore the sheep that snores as it sleeps. Syrup and syllabub and sweet pudding wine will conspire in time to a glutton's decline even if the taste is sublime. Use a white whisk to mix the mixture into a fluffy texture. Sitting here, where the sea is blue, seems better than sitting there when the gas bill is due.

Other Information

Before students are introduced to words like 'except', 'excel' and 'excite' they must first be made familiar with the soft 'c' rule which appears on page 224. Words such as 'excuse' require the 'c' to be sounded as in 'ex / cuse'.

Coach

The Short-cut X

The following spellings sound the same but the one spelled with an 'X' (not cs) is the proper spelling:

eCSpect = eXpect.

The following spellings sound the same but the one containing the 'X' (not gs) is the proper spelling:

eGSam = eXam

Demonstrate the examples above to your student before referring him/her to the diagram on the left. Show your student how each point of the cross represents one of the four letters. Ask him/her to draw it on scrap-paper. Many students will spell a word like 'expect' and still include the 's' (exspect) which is unnecessary as the short-cut 'x' already contains the 's'. Make sure your student understands what 'x' represents.

The letter 'x' makes two common sounds in English: cs / cks: compare 'tax' and 'tacks' or 'gs' as in 'exam', 'exhibit' or 'exile'.

Before starting the spelling columns ask your student to use 'x' in the appropriate words. Words ending in the letter 'x' require 'es' to form the plural: boxes.

Day			Day			Day			Day		
Month			Month			Month			Month		
Pro	x = cs		Pro	x = gs		Spell	Using x Spell		Spell	Using x Spell	
la**cks**			e**x**hort			*mix*			*exam*		
la**x**			e**x**am			*fix*			*exult*		
ta**cks**			e**x**ude			*expand*			*exist*		
ta**x**			g**h**ost			*exhale*			*exotic*		
conve**x**			remove			*expel*			*exact*		
comple**xity**			e**x**ult			*flax*			*existing*		
he**lix**			prove			*relax*			*exile*		
e**x**cuse			e**x**act			*complex*			*exude*		
ve**x**ing			improve			*mixing*			*move*		
e**x**pand			e**x**ist			*sixty*			*prove*		
e**x**tent			where			*convex*			*improve*		
e**x**plode			e**x**hume			*extract*			*exhibit*		

Day				Day				Day				Day			
Month				Month				Month				Month			
Pro				Pro				Spell				Spell			
box				suffix**es**				*toxic*				*relaxes*			
box**es**				export				*spandex*				*exempt*			
fox				equinox				*intoxicate*				*extend*			
fox**es**				Essex				*exhort*				*context*			
relax**es**				convex				*thorax*				*Sax on*			
conflux				thorax				*cortex*				*toxin*			
extent				expect				*exhume*				*ex tinct*			
text				toxic				*excrete*				*mixing*			
vortex				pretext				*fixes*				*anthrax*			
textile				maximum				*syntax*				*fixture*			
influx				explore				*fixative*				*Mex ican*			
flex**es**				expl**o**sive				*beeswax*				*hexagon*			

Day		Day		Day		Day	
Month		Month		Month		Month	
Pro		Pro		Pro		Spell	
squi**re**		expose		st**ore**		*hormone*	
expi**re**		exclude		sc**ore**		*pinafore*	
tribute		belong		enclose		*Marxism*	
inject		testify		explode		*barbarism*	
fax**es**		absentee		justify		*absenteeism*	
exam		junc**ture**		lanyard		*adventure*	
one		punc**ture**		standing		*dandruff*	
stride		expedite		demand		*expresses*	
p**o**lite		explicate		sports		*dismal*	
gone		navigate		electron		*conch*	
come		become		electric		*twitch*	
there		someone		formal		*transpire*	

Coach

More Read and Pronounce Sentences

This is a regular pronunciation exercise. Every word in a line, with the exception of those in grey print, must be read correctly to earn a tick.

You may offer help with the words in grey print. Vowels in **red print** say their **name**.

Do not expect this passage to make sense. Your student must read the words without the aid of contextual clues.

Don't forget: Do not attempt these sentences/lines more than once in the same day!

Read and Pronounce

Continue to take the green pills and take hot baths and you will soon be back to normal. Hang the pic**ture** by the fi**re**; not by the filing cabinet, and make **s**ure it does not get too hot. It was cold by the sh**ore** and the wind t**ore** through the dunes flicking sand into his stinging eyes. The sea splashed his feet and Steve was sorry he was **there** when he could have been somew**here** warm and dry, under the sky, like Texas, Lexington or Mexico. Do not expose your nose to those winds from the North if you are not **s**ure if you can endure the Arctic blasts. Take a thick mix**ture** of tar; black tea; some hot rum; six radishes; and five cloves; nineteen feet of sheep's teeth crushed with three slices of grilled eel and feel much worse than you ever did bef**ore**. Resist the move if you don't approve of it. To improve the recipe: remove the teeth and eel and some of the radish then cook together for twenty minutes at one hundred and seventy degrees. When the smell has g**one** it will not be long bef**ore** you will feel free to sleep on the beach. You will have red cheeks and cold hands but a pair of gloves, sent with love, will help to improve your latest move. Take care over **there** w**here** the snakes in the grass compete with the rats and the br**o**ken glass.

Coach

Has it happened? Simple Past-tense: ed

Read the following sentences:

Sue fix**ed** the shelves.
Jack mend**ed** the car.

Both sentences inform us that something has happened. Sue is not fix**ing** the shelves at the moment. Sue is not going to fix them in the future: she has already fix**ed** the shelves. The same conditions apply to Jack.
The sound made by the letters '**ed**' differs in each word. Listen carefully: the '**ed**' in 'mend**ed**' sounds a little like the '**id**' in 'd**id**'.

To place most words in the **simple past-tense** we add the letters '**ed**' to the end of them.

The silent 'e' makes the preceding vowel say its **name**, therefore, to put silent 'e' words in the past-tense it is necessary to add the letter '**d**' alone:

$$\text{plane} + \text{d} = \text{planed}$$

To stop the power of the silent 'e' from reaching a vowel and making it say its **name**, we must build a barrier by using another letter.

Example: **plan** + **n** + **ed** gives us the word '**planned**' which has a double barrier (**nn**) which blocks the power of the '**e**'. Explain this to your student.

Note: Words like '**b**ang' and '**f**orm' already have two **consonants** after the vowel which protects it from the silent 'e' so doubling is not necessary: b**ang**ed, f**orm**ed.

Day						Both correct to earn a tick!						
Month												
Pro												
plane plan**ed**												
plan plan**ned**												
file fil**ed**												
fill fill**ed**												
di**ve** di**ved**												
cr**ave** cr**aved**												
dru**m** dru**mmed**												
fire fir**ed**												
clo**se** clo**sed**												
lo**ve** lo**ved**												
sh**ove** sh**oved**												
kill kill**ed**												

Day						Both correct to earn a tick!						
Month												
Pro												
peg peg**ged**												
long long**ed**												
hum hum**med**												
hire hir**ed**												
form form**ed**												
lag lag**ged**												
inflame inflam**ed**												
farm farm**ed**												
harm harm**ed**												
endure endur**ed**												
bar bar**red**												
cram cram**med**												

Day						Both correct to earn a tick!						
Month												
Spell												
lob lobbed												
ban banned												
fire fired												
retire retired												
farm farmed *												
charm charmed*												
cure cured												
tan tanned												
prove proved												
starve starved *												
cram crammed												
pull pulled												

Coach: Words marked with an asterisk (*) already have two **consonants** after the vowel.

Other Information

It might seem easier to have the coach pronounce the past tense form of the word rather than use the '+' symbol but that would defeat the object which is to encourage the student to work out the concept of 'simple past-tense'.

Coach

More Work with Past-tense

Column 1: The 'ed' in many words makes the sound 't': Example: 'hiss**ed**' 'march**ed**'.

Column 2: The words have been printed in the present tense + **ed**. Your student must read them in the past-tense: e.g: **demand + ed**: Your student must read '**demanded**'.

Column 3: The spelling column requires the coach to read words in the present-tense which must be repeated by the student in the simple '**past-tense**' form:

1) Coach says "**land**"
2) Student replies "**landed**"
3) Student then writes (spells) '**landed**'.

The words marked + **(p) ed** are reminders that the final letter (**consonant**) must be doubled.

WORD WASP

Day						Day						Day					
Month						Month						Month					
Pro						Pro						Spell	Ask for past tense!				
hiss**ed**						demand + **ed**						*land +*					
march**ed**						recommend + **ed**						*jump +*					
press**ed**						defend + **ed**						*ditch +*					
address**ed**						consent + **ed**						*clap + (p) ed*					
drop**ped**						frost + **ed**						*trap + (p) ed*					
shop**ped**						drift + **ed**						*finish +*					
grasp**ed**						content + **ed**						*sort +*					
undress**ed**						fragment + **ed**						*start +*					
despatch**ed**						inspect + **ed**						*scratch +*					
unpack**ed**						collect + **ed**						*command +*					
unmark**ed**						adopt + **ed**						*import +*					
jump**ed**						invent + **ed**						*infect +*					

Coach

The Digraph er at the End and Within a Word

The letters '**er**' make two sounds: At the end of a word they are barely stressed at all. Listen to the sound that the letters make at the end of the following words:

moth**er**   butt**er**   dinn**er**   min**er**

The sound is little more than a grunt: a short puff of air from the back of the throat! In the majority of cases, where a word ends with this sound, it is usually formed by '**er**'.

In the middle of a word they say '**er**' as in '**ter**m' or 'st**er**n'.

Follow the column guides. Speak clearly.

Day		Day		Day		Day	
Month		Month		Month		Month	
Pro		Pro	**er** as in **tern**	Spell		Spell	
moth**er**		p**er**ch		*bigger*		*fertile*	
bak**er**		**Mer**lin		*tracker*		*terminate*	
driv**er**		s**er**vile		*thicker*		*perfect*	
vip**er**		s**er**vant		*thinner*		*Dervish*	
dinn**er**		m**er**chant		*darker*		*permit*	
simm**er**		st**er**n		*defender*		*perhaps*	
batt**er**		t**er**m		*spider*		*ferment*	
platt**er**		m**er**cury		*banner*		*perplex*	
chatt**er**		int**er**n		*slender*		*perforate*	
sing**er**		t**er**mite		*another*		*terminal*	
mill**er**		exp**er**t		*winter*		*swerve*	
min**er**		p**er**son		*porter*		*server*	

Coach

Introducing Past-tense with er

Column 1: The words have been printed in the present-tense (+ **ed**). Your student must read them in the past-tense: e.g: **splutter + ed**: Your student must read '**spluttered**'.

Column 2 : This exercise will challenge some students who may want to end the words with the letters '**erd**'. The exercise requires the coach to say a word which must be repeated by the student in simple '**past-tense**' form:

1) Coach says "b**o**th**er**"
2) Student replies "b**o**th**ered**"
3) Student then writes (spells) 'b**o**th**ered**'.

Day Month Pro			Day Month Spell	Ask for past-tense	Day Month Pro			Day Month Spell		
splutter + ed			*bother +*		stored			*seg mented*		
batter + ed			*scupper +*		diverted			*tempted*		
hammer + ed			*skipper +*		aspired			*snored*		
cover + ed			*scamper +*		arrested			*starched*		
shatter + ed			*splutter +*		exported			*ventured*		
corner + ed			*blister +*		branched			*obscured*		
gather + ed			*smother +*		postured			*length*		
litter + ed			*shelter +*		sketched			*lengthen*		
glitter + ed			*filter +*		patched			*lengthened*		
tether + ed			*canter +*		expired			*strength*		
foster + ed			*pester +*		involved			*strengthen*		
fluster + ed			*render +*		wheeled			*strengthened*		

Coach

Changing y at the End of a Word

Words which end in 'y' can be extended in much the same way as words which do not, but with one minor difference: we must change 'y' to 'i' and then add the letters 'ed', 'er' or 'es'.

See how the word 'carry' changes when it is extended:

carry changes to carri + ed to form carried
carry changes to carri + er to form carrier
carry changes to carri + es to form carries

Demonstrate the above changes made to the word 'carry' on scrap-paper then begin the exercise.

Don't forget:

Do not attempt the same column twice in the same day: one attempt for one tick or dot! Every word in a row must be read or spelled correctly to gain a tick!

Note: Make sure you have sufficient time to complete the spelling exercise!

Day							Day						
Month							Month						
Pro							Spell						
bully bullying bullied bullies							*marry marrying marries*						
empty empties emptying emptied							*carry carrier carrying carries*						
accompany accompanies accompanied							*deny denies denying*						
magnify magnifying magnified magnifies							*ferry ferried ferrying ferries*						
deny denying denied denies							*cry crying cried cries*						
defy defying defied defies							*try tried trying tries*						
modify modifying modified modifies							*reply replying replied replies*						
simplify simplifying simplified simplifies							*fry fried frying fries*						
dignify dignifying dignified dignifies							*dry dried drying dries*						
signify signifying signified signifies							*defy defied defying defies*						
solidify solidifying solidified solidifies							*comply complying complied*						

Coach: The addition of 'ing' causes problems with words ending in 'y': If we change the 'y' in the word 'frying' to an 'i' the result would be 'friing' which doesn't make sense in English. **Two 'i's cannot meet!**

Day					Day					Day					Day				
Month					Month					Month					Month				
Pro					Pro					Pro					Spell				
terrify					stories					glories					*quidditch*				
terrifying					barrier					gloried					*huskies*				
terrified					pannier					expecting					*drenched*				
terrifies					penny					expected					*hitched*				
edify					pennies					expired					*revolved*				
edifies					entry					desired					*epicure*				
edifying					entries					flexed					*ang strom*				
berry					sentry					complex					*epoxy*				
berries					sentries					exacted					*dervish*				
lorry					folly					extracted					*equity*				
lorries					follies					tireless					*evolved*				
story					glory					primates					*solvent*				

Day		Day		Day	
Month		Month		Month	
Pro		Pro		Spell	**Stress er ***
replied		some		conspire	
marries		**one**		restore	
carrying		some**one**		impure	
party		something		eventful	
parties		somewhere		liberty *	
satire		desire		liberties *	
trenchant		enquire		poverty *	
ditched		enquires		liberate *	
blanket		enquiry		liberated *	
properties		enquiries		identifies	
tropism		calories		rectifies	
green		memory		kinship	
suspires		memories		compete	

Read and Pronounce

"There is nowhere to sit in here for the likes of you", said the lady in the first class seats. Pennies from heaven, money for old rope, cash on the nose, lots of lolly, makes the Empress happier, funnier, fizzier and dizzier. Having carried the empty bucket to the top of the hill Jack refused to carry the full one back down. Jill was very unhappy with Jack's lazy attitude and banged him on the head with the bucket. Jack became very angry but he was too dizzy to reply. Jill was about to apply a small sheet of brown paper to the cut on Jack's head but it was too dry. The wettest thing to hand was a flask of vinegar. This was applied and Jack felt a severe pain which did little for his temper. Jill thought it was time to go and sprinted down the hill. Jack set off but slipped on the wet brown paper and staggered into the path of a lorry. The lorries brakes were applied quickly. The driver, unhappy at Jack's seemingly silly antics, punched him on the nose which bled onto his clean jumper. When Jack's mother saw the dried blood she was sure that Jack had been fighting and confined him to the garden for a month. Jill was denied Jack's company and, as a result, many years later, she married the lorry driver. Such is life!

Read and Pronounce

"But there are no more **seats** on the train and my feet are killing me", replied the

woman with the shopping bags, "and I'm ever so tired. My arms are dropping off!"

It may seem strange but you should know that the vowel sound 'a' after the **consonant**

sound 'w' most often makes the sound of the vowel 'o'.

Coach: Write the word 'wasp' and demonstrate the rule: wasp = wosp

Has **Wa**lly the **wa**sp **wa**shed his wings or has the **wa**rm wind made him lazy?

One must conclude that **wa**sps are rude but not so bees that s**wa**rm on trees.

Was it the **wa**sp that **wa**nted to chase the s**wa**n off the s**wa**mp?

The man with the **wa**rts from **wa**rd three went to **wa**r but **wa**s back in bed when the

woman said, "To whom do these cherries and grapes belong?" "To me", he said with

glee but he **wa**s too late and before long grape seeds and cherry stones were piled upon

his plate. S**wa**p these piles of stones for smiles. Include the man who can s**wa**t the

flies. A consonant is a letter other than a vowel. The vowels are powerful letters.

The letters below are those of our alphabet. The **green** letters are vowel sounds and the

black letters are **consonant** sounds:

a b c d e f g h i j k l m n o p (qu) r s t u v w x (sometimes **y** is a vowel) z.

Other Information

The concept of a letter defying that which a student has already learned ('a' can say 'o') can take some time to instil. Students have already been introduced to the 'ee' rule which is very regular, and proof that one rule works, gives heart when students are struggling with a more difficult one.

Coach

The Sound of the Letter **a** after **w**

The letter 'a' after a 'w' makes the sound 'o'. Listen to the sound in the following words:

w**a**s   w**a**nt   w**a**sh

The sound made by the vowel '**a**' is the same as that of 'o' as in 'd**o**g'.

You have already introduced your student to the double '**ee**' sound.

The letters '**ee**' make the one sound. Listen to the sound in the following words:

st**ee**l   wh**ee**l   gr**ee**d

Day				Day				Day		Tongue *	Day		
Month				Month				Month			Month		
Pro				Pro				Spell			Spell		
was				warp				*swarm*			*washing*		
want				sweetness				*swapped*			*sweeps*		
war				feeling				*wasp*			*watch*		
wart				keel				*wallet*			*feel*		
ward				keen				*warden*			*water*		
wasp				needed				*swamp*			*feeling*		
waft				warranted				*street*			*sheet*		
s**wa**p				seemed				*sward*			*keen*		
s**wa**n				beeswax				*swab*			*been*		
a**wa**rd				warmonger				*feet*			*deed*		
warm				weeded				***th**wart* *			*indeed*		
wand				breeding				*wallaby*			*Walter*		

'a' after 'w' usually says 'o'

Day				Day				Day				Day			
Month				Month				Month				Month			
Pro				Pro				Pro				Spell			
freeze				waft				liberalism				*redeem*			
involve				textile				warlord				*peevish*			
cheese				admire				parakeet				*fleeting*			
boxes				valve				antagonism				*streets*			
canteen				jeered				whimper				*preening*			
galaxy				funky				greedy				*screens*			
seethe				foxes				esteem				*sheer*			
explore				abyss				deportee				*keeping*			
breeze				ghost				republican				*freeze* *			
venture				coffee				wander				*breeze*			
sneeze				toxins				delinquent				*sneeze*			
albinism				toffee				hindered				*squeeze*			

Coach: Spelling: If necessary, remind your student to use double 'ee' and silent 'e'. *

Day				Day				Day				Day			
Month				Month				Month				Month			
Pro				Pro				Pro				Spell			
peeling				enthusiasm				crotchet				second			
defies				washing				quaver				jelly			
denies				complied				speeding				jellies			
streets				someone				disagree				reply			
steered				punctures				filigree				replies			
terrify				proposes				external				dried			
applies				revolved				infernal				drying			
cheek				scorches				amputate				removed			
moved				involved				anatomy				moved			
proved				secluded				dynasties				proved			
second				structured				canned				pedigree			
peltate				strength				segments				peltate			

Coach

The Letters **al** Can Say **or**

If we change the letters '**al**' in the word '**tal**k' for the letters '**or**' we still achieve the right sound for the word:

Example: t**or**k = t**al**k

In many words the letters '**al**' make the sound we associate with the word/sound '**or**'.

Column 3: Ask your student to use silent '**b**'.

Follow the column guides. Speak clearly.

Day		Day		Day		
Month		Month		Month		
Pro		Spell		Spell		Silent b *
talked		talk		talkative		
talking		talked		Dundalk		
walked		talking		limb *		
walking		walking		bomb		
chalk		stalking		lamb		
all		chalk		calling		
ball		ball		fallen		
called		stall		installed		
tall		install		called		
fall		small		thumb *		
stalk		falling		numb		
stalled		taller		crumb		
hall		hall		plumber		

Day						Day						Day						Day					
Month						Month						Month						Month					
Pro						Pro						Pro						Spell	Silent b *				
glee						screen						reviving						*verbose*					
cleft						evolve						exploded						*comprise*					
revise						respite						creeping						*primed*					
des**ire**						ad**ore**						mentholated						*yelped*					
impl**ore**						w**a**lker						practical						*above*					
tinct**ure**						contrite						artic**u**lated						*speech*					
menthol						blend						vamp**ire**						*glove*					
co**mb**						beer						greenfi**nch**						*clim**b** ***					
suspect						cheer						wh**ee**z**e**						*closed*					
clim**b**						linseed						st**a**lker						*bleeds*					
insp**ire**						sweeps						wh**a**cking						*sheen*					
consp**ire**						cheek						enthr**a**lling						*cheered*					

Day						Day						Day						Day					
Month						Month						Month						Month					
Pro						Pro						Pro						Spell					
syntax						deprived						warned						*ex tricate*					
jetty						excuse						plumbing						*ex plicate*					
jetties						exposed						come						*integrate*					
export						adipose						become						*tox ins*					
extent						wanting						welcome						*warping*					
done						warning						signifying						*glossed*					
gone						dwarf						gloss						*replicate*					
wad						expand						emboss						*candy*					
ward						proving						warder						*candies*					
fixed						moving						awarded						*con spired*					
expert						story						coming						*candidate*					
expel						stories						thumbing						*flinching*					

Coach

The Digraphs **ur** and **ir** Make the Same Sound as **er**

The letters '**ir**' and '**ur**' make the same sound and follow the same rule as '**er**' as in '**ter**m' or '**per**ch'.

Listen to the sound made by '**ur**' and '**ir**' in the following words:

bir**d   hu**r**t   fi**r**st   chu**r**n**

Follow the column guides. Speak clearly.

Day				Day				Day				Day			
Month				Month				Month				Month			
Pro				Spell	ir			Pro				Spell	ur		
b**ir**d				*inf**ir**m*				c**ur**l				*p**ur**lin*			
sk**ir**t				*sm**ir**k*				f**ur**bish				*sp**ur**ned*			
sk**ir**ting				*k**ir**k*				m**ur**der				*c**ur**sor*			
sk**ir**l				*th**ir**ty*				m**ur**m**ur**				*h**ur**tful*			
f**ir**st				*d**ir**ty*				b**ur**st				*b**ur**den*			
aff**ir**m				*th**ir**st*				occ**ur**ring				*ch**ur**n*			
fl**ir**ting				*b**ir**ch*				f**ur**niture				*ch**ur**lish*			
sh**ir**t				*besm**ir**ch*				b**ur**ner				*b**ur**st*			
f**ir**m				*conf**ir**m*				c**ur**ve				*urchin*			
squ**ir**m				*sh**ir**k*				t**ur**ning				*f**ur**bish*			
squ**ir**t				*b**ir**th*				sp**ur**ning				*f**ur**long*			
st**ir**ring				*th**ir**d*				ch**ur**ch				*c**ur**ling*			

Coach

The Digraphs ai - ay - ey and Sometimes ei Make the Same Sound: ay as in day.

In words containing 'ai': 'rain' the 'i' is silent but active and makes the 'a' say its name. The same applies to the digraph 'ay': 'day' the 'y' is silent but active and makes the 'a' say its name. This also applies to words containing ei/ey, however, the vowel 'e' will say 'a' rather than 'e', therefore vein = vain and they = thay.

Listen to the sound made by the bold letters in the following sentence: Today the men with grey umbrellas stood in the rain then they went away on a sleigh. As a general rule 'ay' is used at the end of a word and 'ai' is used in the middle of a word. This rule also applies to 'ei' and 'ey'.

You may inform your student which letter combinations (digraphs) are needed to spell the words in each column: ai, ay, ei, ey. The words 'ghost', 'most', 'post' and 'host' are exceptions to the general rule. The 'o' says its name!

Page 146: The Ghost is an important word for our students to learn. We will ask students to 'haunt' words in which case they will be asked to use the letters 'gh'.

Day					Day					Day					Day				
Month					Month					Month					Month				
Pro					Spell	ay				Pro					Spell	ai			
hay					*may*					obt**ai**n					*stain*				
dec**ay**					*dismay*					pl**ai**n					*pain*				
tr**ay**					*display*					p**ai**nful					*pains*				
affr**ay**					*say*					m**ai**n					*train*				
p**ay**					*delay*					dr**ai**n					*fail*				
m**ay**					*saying*					disd**ai**n					*failure*				
pl**ay**					*pay*					t**ai**lgate					*nail*				
sw**ay**					*paying*					fr**ai**l					*trail*				
cl**ay**					*stay*					f**ai**lure					*remain*				
displ**ay**					*staying*					st**ai**n					*drain*				
dism**ay**					*stray*					compl**ai**n					*restrain*				
fr**ay**					*straying*					str**aigh**t					*grains*				

Day				Day				Day				Day			
Month				Month				Month				Month			
Pro				Spell		ey		Pro		The ghost is silent!		Spell		Haunt these words!	
they				convey				sleigh				eight			
convey				survey				neigh				weight			
osprey				they				eight				freight			
grey				grey				eighty				eighteen			
conveying				osprey				weigh				weighted			
conveyed				conveying				weight				freighter			
survey				survey or				freight				weigh			
surveyor				conveyed				reindeer				weighed			
ghost				ghost				weightless				sleigh			
most				most				weighted				neigh			
host				host				skein				weighing			
post				post				weighty				bobsleigh			

Day						Day						Day						
Month						Month						Month						
Pro						Pro						Spell						
thirteen						urbane						dismayed						
further						Whitby						hatchling						
draining						dismayed						sprayed						
straining						delayed						birthday						
surprise						affirmative						starved						
burden						ordained						carved						
straying						exclaimed						starched						
painted						stalking						Monday						
termites						contained						overdue						
perfect						plaintiff						continued						
Washington						explained						Tuesday						
burnished						prevailed						maintain						

Coach

The Ghost (gh) that Haunts English

The word '**ghost**' will play an important role in the spelling of many words throughout The Word Wasp. The letters '**gh**' are **silent** in many words (ri**gh**t) and in others they make the sound '**f**' (rou**gh**) .

You can tell your student that the letters '**gh**' in the word '**gh**ost' **haunt** other words.

In the sentences on the opposite page the letters '**gh**' are **silent**.

Follow the column guides. Speak clearly.

Read and Pronounce

"That is **wh**y more civilized pe**o**ple take the trouble to b**u**y First Class tickets and do not drag **their** family shopping through railway stations", sneered the woman in the blue hat.

If **you** fail to p**o**st the mail then you must take a train to the main station.

If the train comes off the rails you must hide your head and then bite your nails.

In the event of a signal failure; you must wait until the train stops still then take a bu**s** to Notting Hill and if that proves to take too long then take a bike or a bu**s** to Shepherds Bush.

While the train is in the station please refrain from the temptation to move your feet or pick your nose. The trains today are in disarray and very cramped and expensive.

A tray of clay was hard when baked; much too hard to contemplate being eaten by a hungry vul**t**ure. Buttered bones will not tempt them; wings alone hold little meat.

The hail failed to stop the mail from b**e**ing p**o**sted and the details were sent to the men.

If a dog fails to pick up the trail of the r**ei**ndeer y**o**u may feed it some shrimps and snails.

Show him the way to the w**eigh**ing room where he can check his w**eigh**t and h**eigh**t.

A gho**s**t may have a role to play in the way we spell some words today, like w**eigh**t and fr**eigh**t and w**eigh** and sl**eigh**.

Coach

The Diphthong oy - oi

Listen to the sounds made by the orange letters in the following words:

boy deploy coin moist.

These sounds are known as '**diphthongs**'. Demonstrate them on scrap paper before you begin the exercise.

You may tell your student that '**oi**' is used in the middle of a word and, as a general rule, '**oy**' is used at the end of a word.

Exceptions:

royal loyal joyful oyster boycott voyage

Follow the column guides. Speak clearly.

Day							Day							Day						
Month							Month							Month						
Pro	Key Word *						Spell	oy						Spell	oi					
boy KW *							joy							join						
coin KW *							paperboy							coin						
joy Roy							convoy							point						
soil foil							toy							exploit						
toil asteroid							decoy							avoid						
Moira conjoin							employ							spoil						
annoy joint							destroy							toilet						
deploy spoil							destroying							poison						
ploy anoint							coy							hoist						
boil poison							deploy							joist						
moist hoist							envoy							moist						
point joiner							enjoyed							joiner						

Read and Pronounce

Most often, '**ay**', '**ey**', and '**oy**', are used at the end of words but '**ai**', '**ei**' and '**oi**', are used within. Rel**ay** the w**ei**ght of the fr**ei**ght by fax or p**oi**nts on the j**oi**nts will not destr**oy** the b**oi**ls that sp**oi**l one's j**oy**. W**a**lk along the ch**a**lk cliffs to where the ospr**ey** pr**ey**s on fish.

Far from her constant ranting the Crown Prince Henry Jack was considering his exile and how he m**igh**t strike back at that distant empire and those he now disd**ai**ned for taking all his hard work and then with lies procl**ai**m that the Crown Prince was a renegade: his name was cursed and st**ai**ned. However, the Crown Prince was an optimist and some say too l**ai**d-back to hatch dark plots and clever plans with which to attack such powerful foes with hate disposed and whose toxic prose he lacked. He would return to his homeland and without del**ay** to seek his friends and those good men, who would not the Prince betr**ay**. Th**ey** would take the stand; lend a hand; and remove the unjust st**ai**n that sullied all his waking thoughts and caused such acute p**ai**n. But far, far, far aw**ay** the Empress mixed a spell: a mixture so powerful her subjects feared the smell. To be t**ai**nted with its p**oi**son would destr**oy** their nostrils and deliver them to Hellifield: a village near Skipton, North Yorkshire.

Coach: In this exercise the six words or sounds, in a line, must be pronounced correctly to earn a tick. Work from left to right: - - - - - - - - - - - - - ->					Day Month							
> eight	weight	freight	freighter	eighty	eighteen						
> weighed	sleigh	neigh	weighing	sleighing	bobsleigh						
> convey	conveyed	survey	surveyed	surveying	conveying						
> obey	drey	purvey	purveyed	disobey	osprey						
> reindeer	unveil	unveiled	vein	abseil	abseiling						
> elm	elming	whelm	whelming	whelmed	overwhelm						
> ail	avail	ravailed	travail	prevail	prevailing						
> urnit	furnit	iture	urniture	furniture	furnishings						
> amal	algam	malgam	amalgam	malgamate	amalgamate						
> ant	quate	tiquate	quated	tiquated	antiquated						
> ess	itness	witness	witnessing	witnessed	witnesses						
> loy	ploy	loyment	ployment	employment	employing						
> ism	lism	talism	capit	capital	capitalism						
> plasm	doplasm	endoplasm	oplasm	ectop	ectoplasm						

					Day							
					Month							
>	tain	ontain	contain	regained	contained							
>	Spain	stain	taint	restrain	restrained							
>	**aigh**t	**raigh**t	**traigh**t	stra**igh**ten	stra**igh**tened							
>	ay	lay	play	display	displayed							
>	ort	port	ortray	portray	portrayed							
>	erm	termin	extermin	erminate	exterminated							
>	ey	vey	onvey	convey	conveying							
>	oi	ois	oist	moist	moisture							
>	roy	troy	stroy	destroy	destroyer							
>	oint	point	ment	appoint	appointment							
>	oy	loy	ploy	deploy	deployed							
>	ir	irch	birch	mirth	birthday							
>	ur	pur	loin	urloin	purloin							
>	urve	curve	urvey	survey	surveying							

Coach: In this exercise the five words or sounds must be pronounced correctly to earn a tick.

Work from left to right: - - - - - - - - - - - - - >

Day				Day			use: ey - ee	Day				Day				use ai + gh*
Month				Month				Month				Month				
Pro				Spell				Spell				Spell				
burnish				they				complain				container				
bursting				obey				complained				abstained				
thirsty				drey				disdain				Aintree				
parries				grey				first				brainwave				
gantries				weeding				thirst				wardrobe				
terrain				fleeting				thirteen				winched				
serfdom				Greek				failed				drenched				
surveys				agreed				trailed				straight *				
watched				beer				trailing				straighten				
warrant				cheer				straining				straightened				
thrusts				career				remained				constrain				
Turkish				domineer				obtain				disclaimer				

Read and Pronounce

Our words have developed over many hundreds of years and they come from many different lands. The silent 'gh' in our words stems from Saxon England when some words contained a sound like a grunt. We no longer employ that sound but the letters remain. Like an old ghost, they still haunt our words. They will appear in other words which we will learn later. As you work through The Word Wasp you will find that the words in grey print will slowly disappear because you will have learned to spell and read them.

Cleethorpes is a place I know where donkeys feel the strain of carrying children, day by day, in sunshine and in rain. They come by bus, they come by car, and sometimes by fast train to put wet bums on donkeys' backs in order to sustain, the misery of donkeys who never do complain. Many students used to think that spelling was all about memory but now they know that spelling has rules and they are much happier now they know that they are able to learn by the same methods that taught the authors of the Word Wasp, the Hornet and Toe by Toe. Do not destroy the daisies that enjoy the sunshine and the shelter of the cloisters.

Read and Pronounce

Sugar and Sand

To his mum's dismay on holiday

a greedy boy was playing,

quite unafraid,

with a bucket and spade,

on a sandy shore near Cleethorpes.

His mum had said, "Please listen Fred,

before you fill your bucket,

watch the tide by the seaside

it tends to run quite quickly,

along the bay to where we stay

it's silent and quite lethal".

But stolen tarts were in Fred's bag

and nothing could he think of

but trays of sweets and ice-cream treats

and bon-bons by the gob-full.

So when the tide swept by his side

he was jam tarts munching.

He could not run because his tum

was full from over-lunching.

Fred's mum was vexed at this upset

but did expect to see him,

on the next tide, still sat astride,

a sack of apple dumplings.

Read and Pronounce

"Take me to your mother,"

said the spider to the fly.

"I cannot," said the infant

"until my wings are dry."

"Then take me to your brother

it's quite the same to me;

I have not had my dinner

and it's nearly ten past three."

"My brother and mother

are feeding on a toad.

It failed to see the red light

and it stepped into the road.

It's been there for eight days now

and it's smelling rather rank."

It was at this juncture

that the spider's spirits sank.

Then turning white and green again,

threw-up into a tank.

"My wings are now quite dry,"

said the infant cheerily.

"If you would like to creep along

we can meet my family."

"No! No!" said the spider,

"It might seem rather rude

to impose upon your family

as they eat such tasty food!"

Day Month			Day Month		Day Month			Day Month	
Pro	exceptions *		Spell		Spell	exceptions *		Pro	Tongue *
eight			*pusher*		*hover*			disclose	
w**eig**ht			*puller*		*lover*			impose	
fr**eig**ht			*pushed*		*mover*			prose	
h**eig**ht			*anointed*		*boiler*			cl**oth**es *	
vein			*exploit*		*loiter*			praise	
drover			*steroid*		*wanting*			praised	
d**e**coy			*android*		*swamped*			raise	
lay *			*conjoin*		*lay* *			raised	
laid			*describe*		*laid*			trainer	
pay			*training*		*pay*			strainer	
paid			*waiter*		*paid*			spoiled	
say			*strained*		*say*			joiner	
said			*draining*		*said = sed*			moisture	

Coach

Verbs and Adverbs

A **verb** is a '**doing**' word:

running   driving   smiling

A **verb** can be in the **past-tense**:

ran   drove   smiled

An **adverb** describes the action of a **verb**:

The man **was running** (verb) **slowly** (adverb).
The woman **drove** (verb) **quickly** (adverb).

Column 3: Demonstrate how a word which already ends in 'l', (like **hopeful**) still needs another 'l' plus 'y' to change it into the **adverb**: '**hopeful+ly**' or '**playful+ly**'.

Day						Day						Day						
Month						Month						Month						
Pro						Spell	Past tense *					Spell	change y to i add ly *					
joyful joyfully						thankful						angry						
painful painfully						thankfully						angrily *						
slow slowly						lovingly						merry						
quick quickly						bitterly						merrily *						
body bodily						cleverly						happily *						
cheery cheerily						pay *						hopeful						
fresh freshly						paid						hopefully						
hopeful hopefully						say						gainful						
tender tenderly						said						gainfully						
bitter bitterly						avoided						hardly						
wistful wistfully						pointed						playful						
playful playfully						hormone						playfully						

Read and Pronounce

Autumn Bandits

Vespula Vulgaris can be a fearsome beast.	
Of all our native insects	
It's one that's liked the least.	
In June, July, and August	
Wasps struggle to be good.	
By the time October comes around	
The swines are out for blood!	
Open every sandwich.	
Check each can of beer.	
They never fail to find your trail.	
They swarm both far and near.	
They love an ice-cream cornet	
And jam will soon attract,	

Those black and yellow bandits,	
As the dustbin gets ransacked.	
Father hates them more than most	
In fact he's paranoid;	
Attacking them with dishcloths,	
Wet rags and sprays deployed	
But he always seems to miss his foe	
As the kitchen gets destroyed.	
It's called a social insect	
And one can but wonder why	
Such an anti-social animal	
Was given wings to fly.	

Read and Pronounce

The freight train had stopped before the crossing and the man with the flag hailed the man

in the signal box. The other line was blocked by a landslide. Tons of stone, clay and soil

had been moved by the slip and another train was due at any time. The man in the

signal box had to move quickly. He ran along the line to the points and pulled the lever.

The rails clanked noisily as the points moved. Seconds later the train came past the points

then, suddenly, with an unexpected twist, it swung to the left. Tons of steel shifted from side

to side but the train remained on the lines. The man with the flag and the man from the

signal box could hardly contain their joy at seeing the train avoid the landslide.

The next day, before the trains began to run, the entire landslide was cleared hurriedly.

If the paint dries too quickly; make a complaint to the company that manufactures it.

Take the ointment and anoint your joints and other points where painful lumps and nasty

bumps spoil the joys of life. You should be wise and avoid the eyes. Complete the deed

by rubbing the feet with a mixture of linseed oil, garlic and beer. The pain will remain

but the smell will keep away all manner of pests including flies, wasps, and noisy children.

Coach

The Sounds OW and OU

These sounds are also called **diphthongs**. The '**u**' and the '**w**' often represent the same sound in English words.

Listen to the sound of the letters '**ou**' and '**ow**' in the following words:

st**ou**t cl**ow**n tr**ou**t br**ow**n.

Column 3 These words do not contain **diphthongs**. The '**w**' is **silent** and the '**o**' says its **name**:

The words '**sloe**' and '**slow**' should sound the same but there are regional variations.

Follow the column guides. Speak clearly.

Day										Day										Day									
Month										Month										Month									
Pro	silent e *									Pro	KW = Key Word									Pro	ow								
out KW										now KW										slow KW									
stout										cow										blow									
about										clown										below									
shout										towns										hollow									
round										down										growing									
sound										frowning										throwing									
shrouded										gowns										crow									
house *										growl										minnow									
louse *										howler										window									
mouse *										allowed										follow									
pouch										crowned										shallow									
astound										vowels										elbow									

Coach

Spelling with OU - OW and OW

This is a normal spelling exercise. Inform your student of the correct combinations before you start each column.

Reminder: In the 'ow' combination the 'w' is silent and the 'o' says its name.

**Follow the column guides.
Speak clearly.**

Day							Day							Day						
Month							Month							Month						
Spell	ou						Spell	ow						Spell	ow					
spout							now							lower						
trout							cow							show						
moun tain							down							slower						
pound							allow							throw						
compound							clown							flow						
astound							gown							window						
profound							brown							hollow						
ground							frown							below						
couch							drown							glow						
pouch							brow							glowing						
about							how							throwing						
shouting							crown							showing						

Other Information

There are words, fortunately very few, which without a long and protracted discussion of archaisms and old languages, do not lend themselves to easy construction through sounds and rules. A knowledge of the Old Frisian 'wouldest' pronounced 'wowldest' is not going to help students learn how to spell the word 'would' but the 'ou' combination followed by 'l' allows a small point of reference.

Coach

More Work with OU

The first box in the first **Pro** column contains the words **could**, **should**, and **would**. They are related by the 'ou' combination and this is the best place to teach them.

The second box contains words like '**thought**' and '**bought**' where the '**ou**' says '**or**' and the '**gh**' is silent therefore:

bought = **b**ort and **f**ought = **f**ort.

On scrap paper, show your students how to spell these words by demonstrating the '**ou**' combinations followed by the **gh**ost **(gh)**. Make sure you refer to the '**gh**' as "**the ghost**". It is a very useful device!

Orange print has been used to demonstrate where the '**gh**' says '**f**'. The words in the third box, contain words like '**t**ough' and '**co**ugh'.

Follow the column guides. Speak clearly.

Day					Day					Day				
Month					Month					Month				
Pro					Spell		Silent vowel *			Spell		Haunt these words *		
could					astonish					could				
should					astound					should				
would					ex pound					would				
ought					throwing					ought *				
bought					flowing					bought				
brought					trousers					brought				
thought					houses					thought				
nought					bounding					nought				
rough					thousand					rough *				
enough					housing					enough				
tough					house *					tough				
cough					mouse *					cough				
trough					grouse *					trough				

Coach

**Introducing the French Diphthong OU
and More Work with OW**

These words below contain the 'ou' combination
but it makes a different sound. There are very few
words which use this French sound but they are
high frequency words which need to be learned and
this is the best place to deal with them:

yo**u yo**u**th s**ou**p gr**ou**p thr**ou**gh**

Follow the column guides. Speak clearly.

Day				Day				Day			
Month				Month				Month			
Pro	French ou *			Spell	ow / French ou *			Spell	ow / ow		
you *				*powered*				*slow*			
youth				*crowned*				*slowed*			
soup				*powerful*				*glow*			
group				*howler*				*glowed*			
through				*drowning*				*row*			
proud				*bower*				*rowed*			
sounded				*cower*				*snowing*			
found				*towels*				*frown*			
founded				*you* *				*frowned*			
ground				*youth*				*crown*			
rounded				*soup*				*browned*			
jousted				*group*				*flower*			
hounded				*through*				*flowered*			

Coach: If necessary, you may inform your student of the correct letter combinations before he/she starts each column.

Coach

The Return of the Ghost

This exercise will establish the **ghost** as the mechanism for teaching words which have caused spelling difficulties for many students.

Your student must read every word correctly.
Be prepared to offer help with words in bold letters.

Silent letters are highlighted in blue print. Orange print has been used where the ghost says 'f'. Red vowels say their name.

Do not attempt the same line twice in the same day: one attempt for one tick. Dots are not required.

Follow the column guides. Speak clearly.

Read and Pronounce

He thought he saw a ghost through the window of the old house but he was only dreaming.

Our ghosts come from the sounds used by people hundreds of years ago. The letters remain

but the sounds have either gone or they have been softened. Sometimes our ghosts exist to

frighten vowels into saying their names in words such as: sight and might; night and flight;

bright and tight; blight and fight; right and light, though some ghosts are thought to stop some

words ending in 'u' like 'though' and 'through'. Other ghosts will say 'f' in words like enough,

tough, rough, trough and cough. They haunt other words too and we will meet them soon.

Delightfully browned and slightly scorched, not burned, still firm but not curled at the edges, the

baker turns his pancakes nightly, and seasons them ever so lightly. There are smaller ghosts

that come to mind when we look at words sometimes like sign, design and resign. All our

ghosts are quite benign so let us not their name malign.

We do not believe in ghosts. The ones used in the Word Wasp are tricks we borrowed from

history. We believe in the power of vowels. These sounds are very important.

Note: Blue letters are **silent;   red** letters say their **name;   orange** letters say 'f'

Coach

Haunting the Vowel!

The **gh**ost haunts the vowel and makes it say its **name**.

In the **Pro** Column, the **red** letters highlight the vowel **name** and the **silent gho**st, is highlighted in **blue**.

Column 1 Each word must be read correctly to earn a tick.

Do not attempt the same line/column twice in the same day: one attempt for one tick or dot.

Follow the column guides. Speak clearly.

Day		small ghost *	Day		small ghost *	Day	
Month			Month			Month	
Pro			Spell			Spell	
sight delightful			flight sight			plight	
bright plight blight			tight high			lighting	
fight tightly lightly			higher height			slight	
fright might rightly			towels vowels			slightly	
slightly flight sigh			sign design *			delight	
spotlight midnight			resign benign			sighing	
high mighty			assign consign			brighter	
tighten lighten			align malign			fighter	
fighting higher			claim sprain			eight	
sighing tighter			right brightly			weigh	
sign design resign			rain gain			weight	
benign malign *			light nightly			freight	

Coach

Homophones

Your student has been introduced to a number of skills. The next few pages will be devoted to seeing them in action. These exercises will allow for consolidation and the introduction of some **homophones**: words that sound the same but mean different things.

The homophones are highlighted in orange print.

Do not attempt the same line twice in the same day: one attempt for one tick. Dots are not required.

Follow the column guides. Speak clearly.

Read and Pronounce

Go through the garden and try not to stand on the grouped flowers growing by the flour mill

and you ought to warn the youth with the soup that the trousers he bought have worn

through. Eggs have many uses and the baker uses them for baking cakes and pastries.

A fowl is a bird like a chicken or a duck but a foul can mean to break the rules by doing

something sly or nasty. Would the group refuse to put the cold soup in the refuse bin?

A game can be won but one is a number. Four people have come for the show.

We can wander along, around, and about or we can wonder at things which amaze

and astound us. To wonder is to think; to wander is to move slowly and aimlessly.

If you have been fined then you must pay and you find things which have been lost.

We sailed straight through the straits of Gibraltar. He bowled the ball at the bold batsman.

Mind the steps or you might trip. Coal was mined but now it's ripped and spoils the land.

The service duct was very low and the men inside ducked their heads to avoid the spars.

He thought we should tax the rich then put the tacks and nails with the pins and screws.

Could you sail to France to buy wine in the sale or stay at home and pay too much tax?

Day					Day					Day					Day				
Month					**Month**					**Month**					**Month**					
Pro					Pro					Spell					Spell					
destroy					you					*bought*					*deleted*					
enjoyed					youth					*brought*					*foist*					
destroyer					soup					*thought*					*foiled*					
employer					group					*pure*					*embroider*					
acquaint					through					*denture*					*flinches*					
Braintree					tough					*fracture*					*stretches*					
spri**gh**tly					enough					*loiter*					*catching*					
hi**gh**est					rough					*loitered*					*instinct*					
h**ei**g**h**t					cough					*expect*					*instinctive*					
comply					trough					*expecting*					*elected*					
crossfire					thought					*fixture*					*selective*					
carnivore					nought					*mixture*					*theme*					
aper**ture**					brought					*delete*					*extreme*					

Read and Pronounce

Oysters are shellfish that I like to swallow, with pepper and lemon their taste is quite mellow.

You must not crunch them; the effect is revolting! Crabs are much better but require much

messing with sticks and picks; they need lots of dressing. Lobsters are, by far, the most

expensive and with their claws they are quite defensive. They can 'take off' your finger

which seems only right if you're going to boil them: so impolite! Curried or fried, shrimps

can delight but the sight of their skins might give you a fright. Those eyes that look up at

you seem small and bright and they may remind you that once they saw the light.

A seafood platter may contain moist lumps of conger eel or squid with whelks and clams.

Take a walk to the 'chippy' and try haddock, deep fried in batter, it may not remind you that

it was once swimming free in the sea or the lake or the river. Now eat your tea and try not

to quiver at the thought of fresh fish, like huss, hake, haddock, and bass. Just think of liver

with bacon for tea. Does that make you shiver? Fry the dried hake if you make a mistake.

Coach

The Digraph OO: Look at the Moon!

Ask your student to listen to the sounds made by the twin vowels 'oo' in the word 'moon'.

The sound is constant in the first **Pro** column on the opposite page.

Page 182: Listen to the sound of the twin vowels 'oo' in the word 'cook'. The sound is constant in the first **Pro** column.

Note: These sounds are subject to regional variations; particularly in the North. However, this problem arises largely, at the pronunciation / reading level only.

The repeated spellings are necessary to make sure that your student can deal with some difficult words.

Follow the column guides. Speak clearly.

Day						Day						Day					
Month						Month						Month					
Pro	Key Word *					Spell						Spell		French ou *			
m**oo**n KW *						*tools*						*you* *					
fest**oo**n						*mood*						*youth*					
t**oo**						*food*						*soup*					
pont**oo**n						*platoon*						*group*					
d**oo**med						*though*						*through*					
gl**oo**mily						*cooling*						*spoon*					
c**oo**lant						*afternoon*						*loop*					
f**oo**led						*monsoon*						*brood*					
f**oo**lish						*thought*						*groomed*					
p**oo**l						*bought*						*goose*					
t**oo**ls						*stool*						*loose*					
l**oo**se						*spool*						*noose*					
gr**oo**m						*doomed*						*choose* = chooz					

Day							Day						Day						
Month							Month						Month						
Pro	**Key Word** *						Pro						Spell						
cook KW *							soot						*hoodwink*						
floodlight							flooded						*hardwood*						
blood							crooked						*brotherhood*						
hooded							goodness						*cookery*						
though							footpath						*rookery*						
through							rookery						*cooked*						
rook							took						*cooker*						
goods							hooking						*onlooker*						
cooking							wooden						*looked*						
brook							hooked						*crooked*						
shook							stood						*blood*						
goodness							flooding						*understood*						

Day					Day					Day				
Month					Month					Month				
Pro	oose / ose = ooz *				Spell	The ghost says 'f' *				Spell				
floodlight					rough *					should				
brightness					enough *					could				
tightness					tough *					would				
buffoon					cough *					bloomer				
choose *					trough *					moonlight				
loose					though					snooping				
goose					through					foolishly				
lose *					platoon					bloodhound				
tycoon					baboon					floodgate				
blooming					trooper					goodness				
beetroot					trooping					footlight				
loomed					gloomy					goodnight				

Follow the column guides. Speak clearly.

Read and Pronounce

A bull mastiff called Royston was ambling down the Stray,

Rather content to mark his path in the **usual** way,

When along came Homer: a mongrel and a cad,

Who upon seeing Royston was disposed to be quite bad.

Foolishly poor Royston was apt to be unwise:

After burying bones and tasty bits, old pork chops and pies;

He would never fail to mark his trail for a canine cad to find.

A delightful scamp our Homer; an impish plan he chose,

Overtaking Royston by following his nose.

At every tree where Royston's trail hung upon the air;

At every bush and every stump our Homer he was there,

Till he came upon a mound down by the village Green

Where he dug and scraped so fast his tail could just be seen.

And how it w**agg**ed when at last he b**agg**ed the Mastiff's store

And he lifted his **ow**n leg on Royston's pantry door.

Read and Pronounce

The leech is a parasite;

It has a taste for blood.

It sticks itself to healthy things

and drinks more than it should.

Leeches are found far and wide

not only in the water.

Some are found in bank accounts

living off the profits

of others work, from which they shirk,

like slugs from lime or mortar.

Some of them swim all alone,

others swim in shoals

but all of them have sucking gums

which regulate the flow

of life-blood from their victims

from which they don't let go.

Unless of course their greediness

attaches them to one

who has a taste for bloodsuckers

that enter his blue pond.

He will bite them toe and tail

until it's understood

that sucking blood from healthy things

is rude and impolite

and they should drink like others do

or face the angry pike.

Coach

The Sounds Made by the Digraph ea

The vowel combination 'ea' makes three distinctive sounds. Introduce your student to the sounds in the **Key Words** at the top of each column.

In the word '**head**' the '**a**' is **silent** and **inactive** and the '**e**' makes its normal sound.

In the word '**mean**' the **silent** '**a**' is **active** and gives its power to the '**e**' which makes it say its **name**: **mean**.

In just a few words that break the rules the '**e**' is **silent** and the '**a**' says its **name**:

steak great break

Follow the column guides. Speak clearly.

Day		silent a inactive	Day		silent a active	Day		silent e active
Month			Month			Month		
Pro			Pro			Pro		
head KW			mean KW			steak KW		
dead			leaning			great		
instead			clean			greater		
thread			dream			break		
weather			stream			toughest		
breakfast			meat			coughing		
health			streak			roughly		
wealth			bleak			enough		
stealth			leak			host		
peasant			steam			ghost		
feather			dealer			most		
heather			gleaming			post		

Coach

Revision Exercises

The column guides are important. Make sure your student is aware of the necessary sound before you begin each column.

You may inform your student that the words in the box (column 2) end with a silent 'e'.

Page 190: Listen to the sound of the bold letters in the following words: me**asure**, ple**asure**, tre**asure**. They do not say the word '**sure**'. The '**su**' makes a hard form of the sound '**sh**'.

This sound is produced by forming a '**sh**' and vibrating it softly against the roof of the mouth.

m**ea** + **sure**   pl**ea** + **sure**   tr**ea** + **sure**

Homophones, and their companions: homonyms, will always cause problems with this particular rule: **steak/stake**, **grate/great**, **read** and **past participle read**, **lead** and **p.p. led** and **lead** as in pencil or plumbing etc. The pronunciation column will expose some of them.

Follow the column guides. Speak clearly.

Day		ea as in bread	Day		ea as in steam	Day	
Month			Month			Month	
Spell			Spell			Pro	
bread			steamed			utmost	
sweating			teams			hostess	
tread			streaming			ghostly	
stealthy			creamed			outpost	
deathly			screaming			proud	
weather			meaning			shouting	
feather			meaningful			cloudless	
heather			please			mouthwash	
leather			ease			Southport	
steady			disease			enough	
wealthy			crease			toughest	
healthy			lease			roughly	

Day						Day						Day					
Month						Month						Month					
Pro						Pro						Spell					
br**ea**k brake						m**easure**						*treason*					
grate gr**eat**						pl**easure**						*reason*					
st**ea**k stake						tr**easure**						*season*					
st**ea**l steel						steadfast						*heaped*					
f**ea**t feet						threat						*dreadful*					
m**ea**t meet						threaten						*breakfast*					
teem t**ea**m						meanwhile						*instead*					
cheep ch**ea**p						treat						*headlines*					
sea see						retreat						*feature*					
s**ea**m seem						defeat						*pleading*					
been b**ea**n						z**ea**lot						*bleach*					
peel p**ea**l						threading						*cheating*					

Day							Day							Day						
Month							Month							Month						
Pro	tongue *						Spell	use ea						Spell	form the v sound *					
ahead							creature							weave						
close							heater							wove						
closure							bleak							leaf						
deaf							jeans							leaves *						
deafen							beans							wife						
deafening							underneath							wives *						
breath							deadline							self						
breathe *							threat							selves *						
threatening							threaten							wolf						
expose							leading							wolves *						
exposure							weaker							shelf						
treatment							dreaming							shelves *						

Read and Pronounce

The baker will read the book which the butcher read on his seaside holiday in Brighton.

Leaves fall from trees and litter the ground. Steel is a metal but to steal is to take

something which does not belong to you. You can dream about ice-cream or splash in

a stream or you can be mean and keep things for yourself. Have you been shopping for the

French beans? If you clean your teeth with bleach you may not reach your next birthday!

Lean on the lever and steam-clean the carpet. Heal the sick and heel the shoes.

Everyone would like to be healthy, wealthy and wise. In all kinds of weather, leather

weighs more than feathers. Leather can dry in hot weather. Can you measure the

pleasure of swimming and diving in hot sunny weather? Headlines and deadlines make

a reporter's life difficult. She has read the book which he is reading. He led the team

which she is now leading. It seems that the seams of her trousers were splitting.

There are four seasons and thousands of reasons for reading the small print.

Refrain from taking painkillers before you sail because they may fail to sustain your health.

The steak was very tough and the crocodile thought that her teeth were about to break.

"You have overcooked this teacher," the huge reptile growled angrily.

The waiter, an impolite tiger from Bengal, picked his claws disdainfully:

"You complained yesterday that we had left the watch on the referee from Watford."

"That referee lay so heavily after the meal, I was unable to swim for the rest of the day. I could only float on my back and the pelicans jeered at me all day," replied the crocodile.

"Then there was the accountant from Gateshead," the waiter said dryly, "didn't you say that we must have cooked him in his own books?"

"No! That is not quite true. I said that you had cooked him without removing his glasses. Just seeing someone looking up from the plate is enough to put you off meat for life. Why must you insist on cooking them with their heads on anyway?"

"Chef thinks that if you remove the head you lose the flavour," said the waiter.

"Humans don't have much flavour unless they're wearing aftershave or a really strong deodorant," huffed the angry reptile.

"Well if you enjoy aftershave or any perfumed seasoning then humans have to be cooked with their heads on," sneered the tiger.

Day							Day							Day							
Month							Month							Month							
Pro	**Key Word ear** *						Pro	**ear = er** *						Pro							
ear KW *							learn KW *							disappear							
fear							learning							beard							
tear							earning							teardrops							
near							heard							research							
dear							yearn							fearful							
hear							pearl							overheard							
hearing							earnest							gearbox							
clear							yearning							earl							
year							earth							earthen							
rear							dearth							earthquake							
gear							early							nuclear							
appear							search							rehearsal							

Note: Red vowels say their **name**: ear.   Blue vowels are **silent**: **learn = lern.**

Day							Day							Day							
Month							Month							Month							
Spell	**Key Word ear ***						Spell	**ear = er ***						Pro							
ear **KW ***							*learn* **KW ***							bleached							
fear							*learning*							speaker							
tear							*earning*							peaches							
nearer							*earnest*							reaching							
Dear							*yearned*							preaches							
hear							*pearl*							preacher							
hearing							*heard*							teacher							
cleared							*yearning*							repeated							
yearling							*earth*							defeated							
reared							*dearth*							yeast							
gear							*search*							feature							
fearsome							*early*							weakness							

Coach

The Vowel Digraph oa

This is a refreshingly simple rule both to spell and pronounce.

The vowel combination 'oa' works like the silent 'e' in as much as the power moves from right to left:

pole = pol↶e

In the word **coal**, the vowel 'o' receives the power to say its **name** from the vowel 'a' which remains **active** but **silent**:

co↷ al = coal

Demonstrate the rule on scrap-paper and then follow the spelling columns.

Follow the column guides. Speak clearly.

Day					Day					Day					Day				
Month					Month					Month					Month				
Pro					Pro					Spell					Spell				
coat					shoal					*stoat*					*toast*				
roaming					which					*loading*					*coaster*				
coasting					roar					*gloating*					*boastful*				
encroach					when					*oar*					*coach*				
boastful					boating					*roast*					*poach*				
float					ahead					*hoard*					*encroach*				
bloater					moan					*loaf*					*though*				
reproach					while					*loaves*					*thought*				
foal					stoat					*oatmeal*					*enough*				
coaching					remove					*gloat*					*tough*				
gloating					why					*board*					*rough*				
loan					road					*cupboard* *					*soaking*				

Coach: Inform your student that a **board**, upon which we used to hang **cups**, is now a cupboard. The 'p' is silent! *

Day				tongue *		Day				Day			
Month						Month				Month			
Pro						Pro				Spell			
loam	bemoan					hoarded				*clean*			
here	gloaming					bloated				*dream*			
soapbox	moaning					reproached				*throat*			
there	roach					bloating				*moat*			
shoal	toads					coaching				*roasting*			
where	he**al**th					br**ea**kfast				*meaning*			
loach	toaster					broadcast				*steamboat*			
meatloaf	st**eal**th					cloakroom				*a**pp**roach*			
gloat	moat					croaking				*abroad*			
d**ea**fen	w**eal**th					reproachful				*broadloom*			
coax	scapegoat					poaching				*toadstool*			
cloak	hoaxing					coastline				*switchboard*			

Read and Pronounce

Go to the coast where you might be inclined to spend some time watching ships from abroad unloading their cargoes which are loaded on lorries and sent down our roads, while we choke from their fumes.

While roasting a goat, our forbears once thought of drinking mead and making sport. Why swallow the dead wasp on the toast and jam when you can eat the live one on the roasted ham? Yesterday, the goalkeeper wore a charcoal waistcoat under his greatcoat. You may dream of peaches and cream but never once think of toadstools.

Do not boast about your cooking; the toast will burn while you are looking for the butter or the marmalade. Make a sandwich with roast ham; spread it thick with English mustard. Use the powder not the tube but beware the tin marked 'custard'.

Goad a tiger with a stick if you are a lunatic. Encroach upon its quiet repose with a length of oak or rose. Hit it firmly upon its nose or stab it hard between its toes. Take a bold and strong approach; jab it firmly in the throat but put **your** name inside each **shoe**; that's all there may be left of you!

Push a wooden **stake** into the ground. Fillet **steak** is expensive and to cattle: quite offensive! You may cut bread on the breadboard and answer calls on the sw**itch**board.

Coach

The Word - Endings ual and uate

ual

The first vowel, the 'u', takes its power from the second vowel 'a', in order that it can say its **name**. The 'a' is barely stressed but for spelling the coach must stress the 'al' as in 'pal': grad**ual**.

uate

In the 'uate' endings both vowels say their **name**: The 'a' makes the 'u' say its **name** and the 'a' says its **name** because of the final **silent** 'e': grad**uate**

Demonstrate the rule on scrap paper and begin the exercise.

Don't forget: Do not attempt the same column more than once in the same day!

Follow the column guides. Speak clearly.

Day					Day					Day				Beware *		
Month					Month					Month						
Pro					Pro					Spell						
casual					residual					*sens ual*						
manual					mutual					*sex ual*						
sensual					actual					*insin uate*						
unusual					usual					*infa tuate* *						
graduate					factual					*tex tual* *						
insinuate					ritual					*contex tual* *						
extenuate					dual					*pleasant*						
perpetual					rough					*continual*						
eventual					tough					*peasant*						
situate					cough					*enough*						
seasoned					trough					*individ ual*						
reasoned					enough					*punc tual* *						

Coach: The five words or sounds must be pronounced correctly to earn one tick. Work from left to right - - - - - - - - - - - - - >					Day Month								
> casual	casually	casualty	casualties	manually									
> continue	continues	continually	continuing	continued									
> usual	usually	unusual	unusually	factually									
> virtue	virtues	virtual	virtually	habitually									
> leather	feather	weather	heather	weatherboard									
> pound	expound	compound	impound	compounded									
> round	ground	flounder	scoundrel	sounding									
> prow	powder	shower	endowed	elderflower									
> leaning	steamer	streaming	cleaner	released									
> roast	coast	boastful	coastline	oasthouse									
> poach	poacher	poaching	encroached	approached									
> dead	instead	steady	dreadful	breakfast									
> ritual	ritually	mutual	mutually	eventually									
> actual	situate	perpetuate	perpetual	perpetually									

Day			Day			Day		
Month			Month			Month		
Pro	Beware! *		Spell	Beware! *		Pro	ea as in head *	
whether			whelk			mean		
which			which			meant *		
whelk			whether			lean		
white			white			leant *		
whiff			whiff			empty		
whisk			while			emulate		
while			meanwhile			filthy		
meanwhile			when			tilth		
when			whisk			contractual		
what			what			individual		
many *			many *			pleasure		
any *			any			measure		

Coach: Ask your student to take note of the vowel 'a' in the words 'any' and 'many' they take the **vowel sound 'e'**. These are common words which break the rules. *

Read and Pronounce

Entertaining when it's raining
around our father's barbecue,
burning burgers, heavens open
in continual murky moments,
spitting feathers over charcoal,
sister Daisy waits for food.
Next door neighbour passing chicken
leg still frozen speaks to Daisy:
"think this chicken's not cooked through!"
Sees the cat there, Father's treasure,
stealthy feline, stealing morsels,
digging seedlings, chomping songbirds,
steals the chicken leg from Daisy,
in the way that fat cats do:
resentful, haughty and ungrateful:
the Burmese mouser: Montague.
Father's smoke filled eyes did water
and his frozen chicken too,
over burgers, over salad,

over sandwich, over hot dog,
into mustard, over custard,
into Mrs. Thrumstop's dressings,
into that to be avoided: Mrs. Glumstrum's
cheese fondue.
Very soon the sun was setting
over garden party revellers,
and those locked inside the loo,
throwing up and shouting "chunder."
In the bushes gripping tummies,
friend and relative continued puking,
but not the hated Montague.
On his back, his form contorted,
Father's treasure for good measure
had stolen more than he could chew!
Quite dead and well stiffened
full of fowl and salmonella
lay the Burmese fat cat:
Montague!

Read and Pronounce

When spores and pollen rode the bree**ze**	As Duncan lay quite fast asleep	
Mr. Duncan Rees from Leeds	For the super-glue she reached.	
Had a tendency to snee**ze**.	His snores upon his lips would flutter	
Much to his wife's dismay	"But not for long", she was heard to mutter.	
His teeth would often fly away.	Much has changed for Duncan Rees:	
At gr**ea**t speed and without warning,	No longer will his mighty snee**ze**	
His dentures left his lips one morning;	Propel his **g**nashers through the air.	
Never to be seen until	His teeth redeemed from up the tree	
Mrs. Rees from her window sill	Sit grinning from the mantelpiece.	
Spied the teeth well out of reach	Now Duncan sleeps in mute repose	
Smiling from a nearby tree.	Emitting through his bunged-up nose	
Mrs. Rees began to seeth**e**;	**O**nly modest little snores.	
The problem of her husband's teeth	Life for Mrs. Rees is sweeter	
Had r**i**sen again and could be seen	Much more **w**holesome and completer	
To effect her mood like kerosene	With all the power she can muster	
Unwisely used on barbecues:	With hint of pepper and feather duster	
His naked gums had lit her fuse.	She plays upon poor Duncan's fears:	
A terrible plan she now perused.	To have his brains blown through his ears!	

Coach

The Letters air - are as in fair - fare

There are many homophones, (words which sound the same and mean different things) involved in this exercise. For instance:

> **h**are - a rabbit like animal

> **h**air - which covers our head

It is important, when spelling, that your student understands which combination of letters: 'air' or 'are', we are using because they both sound the same.

On the opposite page in the **Pro** and **Spell** exercises, the words contain the sound 'air' as in 'chair'. The words in the **Pro** and **Spell** exercises on **page 208** contain the sound 'are' as in 'care'.

The **Pro** exercise on **page 209** contains an explanation of the possessive pronoun 'their'. It doesn't matter if your student doesn't understand it. Be assured: one day he/she will. Once your student has become familiar with the rules and structures of words; he/she will then be receptive to other ideas.

Follow the column guides. Speak clearly.

Day				Day				Day		
Month				Month				Month		
Pro	**Both correct to earn a tick!**			Pro	**Both correct to earn a tick!**			Spell	**using air**	
fairest flair				chaired impaired				*repair*		
aired aircraft				stairs corsair				*dairy*		
chair upstairs				air fairground				*hairy*		
fair fairway				stairway airman				*eclair*		
dairy dairies				solitaire Claire				*downstairs*		
hair paired				unfair airport				*fairway*		
armchair lair				airtight airborne				*fairies*		
airy hairy				impairing airwaves				*armchair*		
airtight eclair				chairman airmail				*debonair*		
Airedale pair				despair impair				*despairing*		
cairn bairn				airliner airbus				*solitaire*		
fairy fairies				affair despairing				*repaired*		

The letters **eir** can also make the sound **air** as in **heir** and **their**

Day						Day						Day					
Month						Month						Month					
Pro	Three correct to earn a tick!					Spell	use are					Spell	use are				
compare flared Kildare						rare						declare					
blare square spared						rarely						warehouse					
stare stared hardware						welfare						scared					
flare ware warehouse						glared						nightmare					
dare mare hectare						software						Kildare					
care scare welfare						snare						careless					
bare beware careful						ensnare						careful					
hare aware rainware						fanfare						Spell	use ear *				
scared declare careless						barefoot						pear *					
spare unaware software						prepare						wear					
glare prepare parent						carefree						bear					
share shared rarely						barely						tear					

Read and Pronounce

There are many words which sound the same but they are spelled differently. We can eat a pear or wear a pair of socks. He stares at the stars and walks up the stairs. We can run like a hare and lose our hair as we get older. A hare is a rabbit-like animal which is covered in fine hair which keeps it warm. The letters 'eir' say 'air' and if we add an 'h' to the front, which makes 'heir', it will still sound the same as the word 'hair'. We can brush our hair but an heir is someone who will possess something. Someone who will inherit something is an heir. The word 'there' is about a place. The word 'their' is about owning something; it contains the word 'heir'. There will be a meeting here so put their hats and coats in the cloakroom. This belongs to them therefore it is theirs. The word 'their' is possessive: It is concerned with ownership. It needs an heir! We must pay our fare when we take a bus to the fair. The hare sniffed the cold morning air which blew through its thick hair. It was cold there and we had to share our spare clothes with their children. It was only fair!

Coach

Words Ending: **er - ar - or - our**

The letters '**ar**', '**er**', '**or**' and '**our**' can make the same unstressed sound at the end of a word.

Listen to the following word endings:

> bigg**er** small**er** coll**ar** doll**ar**
> act**or** trem**or** flav**our** col**our**

Demonstrate these endings on scrap-paper and then begin the exercise. Be sure to tell your student which ending to use.

Follow the column guides. Speak Clearly.

Day				Day				Day				
Month				Month				Month				
Pro				Spell		our - or		Spell		er - ar		
anger bigger barrister				*vigour rigour*				*foster*				
lavender Gulliver deliver				*favour flavour*				*blister*				
banner summer tender				*colour harbour*				*trainer*				
polar solar molar				*honour splendour*				*joiner*				
secular lunar regular				*glamour clamour*				*grammar*				
pillar tartar angular				*parlour savour*				*popular*				
vendor regulator castor				*humour candour*				*burglar*				
factor vector inventor				*ejector victor*				*Cheddar*				
traitor rector adaptor				*tractor adaptor*				*jugular*				
candour colour honour				*factor rector*				*jocular*				
labour rancour valour				*sector doctor*				*secular*				
parlour harbour humour				*emperor actor*				*annular*				

Other Information

Get, give, begin, forgive, forget, burger, are common words where the soft 'g' rule does not apply. They are basically German words with origins in our language which pre-date the Norman Conquest which introduced the 'soft g'.

Coach

The Soft Sound of the Letter **g**

The letter '**g**' before '**i**', '**e**' or '**y**' makes the sound '**j**'. There are exceptions. The common exceptions are:

get   give   begin   forgive   forget   burger

This is an important exercise and once the rule is mastered; your student's spelling vocabulary will have been greatly enriched. Listen to the sound made by the '**g**' in the following words:

gin   engine   gent   gene   gym   gyrate

The '**g**' is making a sound which we normally associate with '**j**'.

The rule is: '**g**' followed by '**i**', '**e**', or '**y**' says '**j**':

Gypsy = Jipsi

Look at the word **Gypsy:** The '**y**', acting as '**i**', makes the '**G**' say '**J**'! The '**p**' and the '**s**' make their normal sound and the final '**y**' says '**i**'.

gym = jim   ginger = jinjer   gent = jent

Day							Day							Day						
Month							Month							Month						
Pro							Spell							Spell						
Gypsy							*agitate*							*gesture*						
gent							*agile*							*collar*						
a**ge**nt							*agent*							*gene*						
enga**ge**							*gender*							*dollar*						
aller**gy**							*fragile*							*genetic*						
a**gi**le							*beggar*							*polar*						
a**gi**lity							*lunar*							*gin*						
fra**gi**le							*gent*							*molar*						
gender							*calendar*							*ginger*						
gymslip							*magic*							*solar*						
gin**ge**r							*tragic*							a**ll**er**gy**						
plu**nge**r							*register*							*gerbil*						

Day		Day		Day	
Month		Month		Month	
Pro		Pro		Spell	
germ		engineer		*congest*	
gyrate		though		*logic*	
energy		tough		*logical*	
synergy		cough		*Angela*	
fringe		danger		*Angelo*	
stringent		strange		*gelignite*	
magical		strangest		*ger minate*	
angelic		manger		*le thar gic*	
gem		arrange		*large*	
pungent		ranger		*digest*	
gorge		stranger		*charge*	
George		change		*hinge*	

Gradually, a range of strange things began to happen and there was a danger that the dark stranger would find the ginger biscuits which were hidden in the pleasure gardens. Onions are pungent; they will make you sneeze but not cough in any orthodox way, though seeds in the breeze, before they germinate, may terminate their journey by sticking in your windpipe. You may ingest them; not digest them. They tend to pass through you. How rude!

Angela and Angelo were both allergic to Gerry. He was often lethargic and would lay on his back, eating oranges, which were provided, after peeling, by Gemma the gymnast from Brighton.

The regiment was outraged when the regimental goat was eaten by the General. Brigades and platoons were plunged into mayhem when it was heard that he ate a third of the animal himself. "Haul him before a magistrate," said the irate men. The General remained aloof: "We went into battle yesterday and the goat was killed. It would have been a pity to waste him." "What about us?" raged the soldiers. "If you die; there will be far too many bodies for the cooks to deal with," returned the General.

Coach

Build a dam with a d!

You have seen how a '**j**' sound at the end of a word can be formed by '**ge**'. However, the '**e**' does not lose its power to affect the vowel to its left. It is **silent** but **active**!

Example: age page sage

If we need to stop the '**a**' from saying its **name** we must build a barrier and **dam** the influence of the final '**e**'. We use the letter '**d**' for that purpose. The '**d**' remains **silent** and the vowel keeps its **sound**. However, although the '**e**' is **silent** it remains **active** and makes the '**g**' say '**j**'.

Example: **ba**dge - remove the '**d**' and '**a**' will say its **name**: **bage**.

In words like ba**rge** and lu**nge**, the vowel is already protected from the '**e**' by the **consonants** '**r**' and '**n**' respectively.

The '**idge**' sound at the end of one-syllable words is formed with a silent **d**: bri**dge**, fri**dge** and in words with more than one syllable ending with an '**idge**' sound; we use the letters **a g e**: vill**age** cabb**age** man**age** sav**age**. There are exceptions but very few:

porri**dge** - cartri**dge** - partri**dge**.

Don't worry if this seems like a great deal to take on board. The exercises will explain it all.

Day									
Month									
Pro									
sage									
badge									
huge									
lodge									
page									
budge									
stage									
grudge									
nudge									
oblige									
gadget									
refuge									

Day								
Month								
Spell	**use 'd' for dam**							
lodge								
wedge								
judge								
Nigel								
sedge								
dredge								
wage								
stage								
oblige								
gadget								
page								
fudge								

Day								
Month								
Pro	**age = idge**							
ridge								
carnage								
pillage								
bridge								
manage								
lovage								
fridge								
baggage								
luggage								
ravage								
village								
savage								

Day		Day		Day	
Month		Month		Month	
Spell	age = idge	Pro		Spell	
bridge		barge		Stonehenge	
cabbage		forge		revenge	
plunge		lunge		avenger	
badge		gorge		bulge	
nudge		sponge		indulge	
fridge		danger		gorge	
garbage		divulge		George	
ridge		indulge		danger	
village		large		stranger	
cringe		arrange		trudge	
avenge		expunge		budget	
grudge		strange		arrange	

Read and Pronounce

In the dark ages, Viking raiders would raid and pillage the villages along the east coast.

Walk up the stairs and stare out of the window. Watch the rabbits damage the leeks and cabbages.

Cut the cloth with a pair of scissors and savour a pear before its flavour becomes impaired and much too ripe to eat. Take advantage of the very rare warm and sunny weather. A gradual approach to spelling, using rules and structure, I declare, is much better than trying to guess or remember them from a long list which contains lots of generically unrelated words.

A flare is a rocket that lightens the sky. Flair is a talent or skill. Walk along the ridge to a village.

A manual worker has just as much right to use a pen as a teacher or a doctor.

Individual pies can make your eyes water if they are covered in pepper or chillies.

According to the engineer, the loudest account of events is usually the least factual.

Beware of the jackals that gather like vultures; they steal the meat from the hand of their brother.

Is the Royal Dowager Duchess of Dyslexia deluded? Why has the Crown Prince been excluded?

George forged ahead through the gorge but was then disgorged into a large barge where the man with the bulging wallet was in charge of the bilge pumps which were purged on a daily basis.

Read and Pronounce

The bear could no longer endure the cold. She felt quite bare in the cold weather. Bruno, her estranged husband, didn't know whether to hide from the weather either. He was still on good terms with his former partner and he had bumped into her by accident as they were raiding the garbage cans outside the hunting lodge. "What a very poor diet these hunters have!" said Angela. "They come here hunting bears so they can mount heads on a wall. Our heads! Then they eat this garbage: pizza, burgers, and all the usual junk food. I mean, there are deer, rabbits, and even pheasants out there! Why pick on us? They don't even like bear meat!"

"Which reminds me!" said Bruno, "Where are they?"

"Sleeping it off! They haven't seen a bear all day. I know! I followed them! They left a trail of empty beer cans right through the forest."

"Did they drink it all?" enquired Bruno.

"No! There is a case by the edge of the river. They were too drunk to carry it over the bridge."

"Tell you what Angela! I've been thinking. I'm ready to hibernate. In fact I've just about finished digging my new pad just above the snow-line. How about you and me having a little meal for two before we get our heads down for the winter?"

"What! Just you and me? Are you sure? Well maybe! But we had better not argue."

"Well! I thought if you haven't dug yours yet you might think about staying a while."

"You always were an old romantic. Go get the beer; I'll bring the pizza."

Read and Pronounce

Her Royal Highness, the Empress, has been troubled by double vision for many years. After a severe bout of seemingly unprovoked anger, she stormed out of the dining room, took the wrong alternative and fell, headlong, down the steeply pitched staircase. Her horrified subjects took their leave rather quickly; leaving her to curse and swear at her own misfortune. There was little choice: Their fate would have been terrible had they been present at her loss of dignity. Their only choice was to flee while their heads remained on their shoulders. Any remaining thoughts that she might cool her temper with ice-cream, a delicacy of which she was extremely fond, soon disappeared. When asked to savour a new flavour several hours later, she replied with vigour that any peasant known to have been present at the time of her accident would be sent to the 'Tower', tossed in flour, toasted and roasted, their heads put on stakes, their other bits minced and despatched to the fringes as parcels of meat to feed the dogs and wild beasts that feast on the pheasants and sometimes those peasants who stray from the shelter and safety of their homes to tend to their sheep.

The judge **was** sleeping on his bench.			The walls w___ bare and stripped of paint.		
The defendants **were** swearing oaths in French.			The cat w___ feeling rather faint.		
Not many people **were** signing the pledge.			She sank her teeth in George's bottom.		
The General **was** inspecting the men.			I think he will ride cats no more!		
The men **were** not expecting the General.			One team w___ playing.		
The clouds **were** gathering in the sky.			The players w___ playing.		
The sun **was** shining in my eyes.			The village blacksmith w___ taking snuff.		
The wasps **were** swarming on the marmalade.			The flavour of the sweet w___ horrid.		
His mother **was** dancing upon the stairs.			The women on the ridge w___ very angry.		
His father **was** watching in disbelief.			The refugees w___ tired and hungry.		
George **was** sitting on the cat.			Disease w___ spreading through the village.		
The cat **was** looking quite annoyed.			Butter mountains w___ melting in the hot sun.		
The bears **were** fishing in the pond.			**You were very unpleasant!**		
Two brown bears **were** eating pears.			**The word you breaks the rule.**		
Where **were** their clothes?			**It can apply to one or both of you.**		

Coach: Ask your student to read the first word in bold print and then the corresponding phrase.		Day Month							
Pro		Pro							
pair: a pair of shoes		danger							
pear: a fruit that we eat		strange							
bear: an animal that lives in the forest		stranger							
bare: to be without clothes		range							
wear: as in clothes that we wear		arrange							
where: a site where something exists or happens		hinge hinged							
hair: that grows on your head		cringe cringed							
heir: someone who will own something		forge forged							
stairs: the ones we climb to bed		large enlarged							
stare: to look intensely		lunge lunged							
their: something that is owned by people		plunge plunged							
there: somewhere to go or to leave		charge charged							
Look for the **heir** in **their** if it belongs to someone!		stage staged							

Coach

The Soft C Rule

So that's why we have the letter K!

In the basic sounds we learned that both '**c**' and '**k**' make the same sound in words like **cat** and **kipper**. However, if we use a '**c**' before an '**i**', '**e**', or '**y**'; the sound changes to '**s**'. Listen to the sound of the letters '**c**' and '**k**' in the following words:

cent **ci**vil **cy**mbal **ci**ty **ke**nt **ki**d hus**ky**

If we need to form a '**c**' sound before '**i**', '**e**', or '**y**' we must use a '**k**'.

The '**s**' at the end of a word can often say '**z**' (hi**s**) but '**ce**' always makes the soft sound of '**s**'.

Example: **hens** v **hence**   **fens** v **fence**
See advice and advis(**z**)e **column 4.**

Follow the column guides. Speak clearly.

Day						Day						Day				split sounds *		Day				Greek / Latin *	
Month						Month						Month						Month					
Pro						Pro						Spell						Spell					
cell						dance						*lance*						*civic *|					
kelp						kipper						*chance*						*civilize*					
cent						chance						*France*						*concentric *|					
city						glance						*glance*						*bounce*					
race						romance						*dance*						*ounce*					
concede						produce						*village*						*flounce*					
cedar						finance						*romance*						*trounce*					
fence						ounce						*celery*						*announce*					
cellar						bounce						*celebrate*						*advice*					
cynic						trounce						*embrace*						*advise*					
except						flounce						*ex cept *|					*pacify*						
excite						cider						*ex cite *|					*placid*						

Coach

Double CC

Many words use a double 'c' (cc).

If the letters 'cc' are followed by 'e', 'i' or 'y' then the first letter says 'c' as in 'car' and the second 'c' forms the **soft** 'c' sound. Listen to the following word: ac cent.

accent = acsent

It is the **soft** 'c' rule once more. It just seems complicated by having twin letters:

ac cident = **ac s**ident

In the **Pro** column the 'c' in bold print must be pronounced as 's'.

Follow the column guides. Speak clearly.

Day						Day					soft c	Day					a mixture			
Month						Month						Month								
Pro						Spell						Spell								
ac**c**ept						*ac cept*						*accord*								
ac**c**ord						*ac cede*						*occur*								
ac**c**ent						*ac cident*						*account*								
ac**c**olade						*oc cident*						*accumulate*								
ac**c**ede						*ac celerate*						*accomplish*								
ac**c**use						*ec centric*						*necessary*								
ac**c**ident						*ac cent*						*occupy*								
oc**c**ur						*ac cess*						*succulent*								
ec**c**entric						*suc cess*						*suc cessive*								
hic**c**up						*suc ceed*						*accuse*								
poli**c**y						*oc ciput*						*recite*								
vac**c**inate						*suc cinct*						*ac cip itral*								

Coach: Ask your student what the word 'necessary' would say with a double 'c' (nec **c**essary)!

Day							Day								Day						
Month							Month								Month						
Pro							Pro								Spell						
Kevlar							ri**ce**	**s**							*trace*						
hence							ri**se**	**z**							*specific*						
trance							advi**ce**	**s**							*peace*						
balance							advi**se**	**z**							*atrocity*						
mince							pri**ce**	**s**							*electricity*						
kitten							pri**s**ed	**z**							*spliced*						
sentence							embrace								*recital*						
France							placid								*nice*						
advance							Pacific								*fallacy*						
distance							pacify								*vicinity*						
freelance							specify								*censure*						
convince							lance								*quince*						

Read and Pronounce

Give notice to the service of the menace which stems from the palace of the Empress where a poisoned chalice will be offered with malice to those who challenge the degrees and edicts of the Royal Office. It has long been the policy in that region to exile or send to the foreign legion all those who offend against her religion. A decimal point on a bank balance can make the difference between joy and misery. Acceptance of advice before an advance may not lead to the chance to advise the woman from France to think twice; so take advice and prise the ice from the frozen rice or pay the price with a head-full of lice. You will have success with the correct shampoo. Soap alone will not do and consider not a tube of glue. In the precinct, a distinct smell of tar and gin floats in and out of cellars grim where heads are shaved and bodies waxed and fleas and mice live free from tax. The recent rains have washed the plains and clouds of flies have advanced within reach of the crowded beach. Are eccentric people more accident prone? Access to the press was not succinct so vaccinate the occupants accordingly. Convince the man from the palace that the women in the province are advancing quickly.

Reminder: You can assist your students with words in grey print without incurring a dot!

Coach

More Soft C

This is a pronunciation and spelling exercise.

Note: The letters '**i c e**' at the end of a word of more than one syllable **usually** makes the sound '**iss**'.

Examples: off**ice** = off**iss**   serv**ice** = serv**iss**

Words in **column 4** ending with the letters '**a c e**' must have the '**a**' stressed. Ask your student for the proper pronunciation immediately after he/she has spelled the word concerned.

Follow the column guides. Speak clearly.

Day					Day					Day					Day				
Month					Month					Month					Month				
Pro					Pro					Spell					Spell				
malice					edifice					ice					malice				
notice					justice					nice					notice				
Alice					stalking					lice					novice				
novice					hallway					price					Alice				
chalice					officer					slice					chalice				
coppice					tallboy					splice					concern				
cornice					lattice					thrice					cornice				
avarice					chalked					twice					office				
office					walking					advice *					farce				
cystic					necessary					advise					lattice				
palace					appalled					device					palace				
menace					service					devise					menace				

Coach: The 'soft **c**' *always* makes the soft sound of the letter '**s**' (advi**ce** and devi**ce**), however, 'advi**s**e' and 'devi**s**e' end with hard **z** sounds. *

Coach

The Different Sounds and Uses of CC and CK

The exercise opposite is a reading only exercise. We need students to understand why we use both the letter '**k**' and the combination '**ck**'.

The letter '**k**' serves to provide a '**c**' sound before '**e**', '**i**' and '**y**'. It cannot be used in double combinations (**kk**) because that would break the rule we wish to uphold: Usually, '**k**' can only be used before '**i**', '**y**' and '**e**'.

Later it will be **silent** before '**n**'. It can be used to form the end of words like '**bank**' as there is the potential to extend the word '**bank**' to '**banker**' or '**banking**'. In each case, the first letter of the extension is '**i**' or '**e**'.

The sound '**bak**' sounds exactly the same as '**bac**' but if we try to extend '**bac**' to form the word '**backer**' without adding the '**k**' we can only achieve the sound '**bacer**', which rhymes with '**racer**'.

If we doubled the '**c**' we would have the sound '**baccer**' (which would say '**bacser**') because the '**e**' would change the second '**c**' to '**s**'. We have to provide a double barrier without altering the sound of the vowel or the sound of the '**c**'.

We could try to use a single '**k**' but that would produce '**baker**' and we cannot double the '**k**':

The solution is provided by the combination 'ck': 'backer'!

Read the lines from left to right. The first section demonstrates how twin **consonants** act as a shield and determine whether a word will contain a **vowel sound** or a **vowel name**.

The yellow sections contain spelling mistakes which can, and **must be read**, in order to fully understand the rule.

Coach: Work from left to right. All six words, correct and misspelled, must be pronounced correctly to earn one tick. Work from left to right - - - - - - - - - - - - >	Day Month								

We have already learned that we need to double **consonants** to stop vowels from saying their **names**.

hop	hopping	hopped	hoping	hoped	hope
slop	slopping	slopped	sloping	sloped	slope
tap	tapping	tapped	taping	taped	tape

We have already learned that '**c**' before an '**i**', '**e**' or '**y**' makes the sound we usually associate with '**s**'. Instead of double '**cc**' we use the combination '**ck**'. This allows us to extend words with '**ing**', '**er**', or '**ed**'.

cit	cing	ceg	kit	king	keg
bac	bacing	baccing	back	backing	backed
doc	docing	doccing	dock	docking	docked
roc	rocing	roccing	rock	rocking	rocked

Any root word ending **consonant** '**c**' sound must use '**k**' alone because they too can be extended by '**ing**', '**er**' or '**ed**': **link risk park thank**

marc	marcing	marccing	mark	marking	marked
parc	parcing	parccing	park	parking	parked
thanc	thancing	thanccing	thank	thanking	thanked

Other Information

Just for the record: 'guard' and 'guardian' are variant forms of the old Northern French and Anglo Norman word 'wardein' (warder) which is a variant of the old French word 'guarden' (gwarden) hence: **guardian**.

I am the g**u**ard and this is my shield!

Coach

The Vowel U is the Guard!

The **silent** letter 'u' protects the 'g' from the power of the vowels 'e', 'i' and 'y'. If we want the letter 'g' to make its normal sound before the letters 'e', 'i' and 'y' we place a shield (u) between the letter 'g' and the vowel. The 'u' remains **silent** but protects the sound of the letter.

The sound made by the following letters: '**gest**' is the same as the word '**jest**' but I am expecting g**u**ests for dinner!

As the 'u' is a guard we find it in its own name: g**u**ard. A g**u**arantee is a g**u**ard too!

The 'u' performs the same role for soft 'c': cir**cu**it - bis**cu**it.

The 'u' allows the 'c' in each word to say 'c' as in '**car**'.

Day		Day		Day	beware *	Day	beware *
Month		Month		Month		Month	
Pro		Pro		Spell		Spell	
guide		vague		gender		brogue	
guest		ingest		gentry		vogue	
guard		plague		damaged		guard *	
garden		guitar		managed		garden	
guarantee		fragile		outraged		caged	
biscuit		guile		guarantee *		biscuit	
circuit		guise		savaged		circuit	
guess		original		ravaged		guitar	
Guilford		beguile		cent igrade		gastric	
guilt		disguise		pacify		guilt	
guilty		tragic		pacified		specify	
vogue		beguiling		decimate		guess	

Reminder: Blue letters are **silent guards** and **red** letters say their **name**!

Day					Day					Day				
Month					Month					Month				
Pro					Pro	age says idge				Spell				
agile					congested					*age man**age**ment*				
bro**gue**					ju**d**gement					*harbinger agent*				
ginger					Egypt					*messenger plague*				
le**d**ger					Gypsy					*original pledge*				
thought					g**y**rate					*ginger biscuit*				
bought					pass**age**					*guitar circuit*				
guy					mess**age**					*originate guide*				
gorilla					man**age**					*algebr**a** general*				
guerilla					eight					*disguise rogue*				
algebra					weight					*Guinness guard*				
general					**height**					*Gypsy Egypt*				
fugue					obli**g**e					*gerund guy*				

Read and Pronounce

Words which have entered our language from the tribes of the North German Plain do not follow the rule for 'Soft G': give, begin, forget, burger, forgive, get. There is a debate about the term 'Gypsy': Some people think that it should be spelled with 'i': Gipsy. Other people make the point that travelling people originally came from Egypt and the word 'Gypsy' came from a short form of the word 'Egyptian'.

In some words 'u' can make the same sound as 'w'. This happens with words containing 'qu'. The 'q' makes the sound 'c' and 'u' makes the sound 'w'. Listen to the sound made by 'qu' in the word 'quick', then listen to the sound made by the letter 'u' in the words 'penguin', 'suite' 'persuade', 'language', 'linguist' and 'linguistic'. We will meet these words again. Now you have reached this stage of the book you may have noticed that your reading skills have improved with your spelling skills. Some people think that spelling and reading are **separate** skills. What do you think? **We think you are getting the message!**

Coach: The letter 'u' can say 'w': quick quit penguin linguist etc.

Coach

Dams D and Guards U

The exercise on the opposite page has been designed to both clarify and instruct. The instructions regarding soft 'g' have now been augmented by the use of the **dam** 'd' and the **guard** 'u'.

The **dam** 'd' allows the vowel to keep its sound.
The guard 'u' protects the 'g': it allows us to make a 'g' sound before 'i', 'y' or 'e'. Without the guard; the letter 'g' would say 'j'.

The same rule applies to bis**cuit** and cir**cuit**.

Remove the guard 'u' and the pronunciation changes:

biscit = bissit / circit = sirsit

Coach: Work from left to right. All six words, misspelled and correct, must be read correctly to earn a tick. This exercise will clarify whether your student understands the rules which have governed the previous exercises.					Day						
					Month						
> gess	guess	gest	guest	gilty	guilty						
> gide	guide	gise	guise	gitar	guitar						
> Gilford	Guilford	gerrilla	guerrilla	disgise	disguise						
> gidance	guidance	Gernsey	Guernsey	vage	vague						
> roge	rogue	voge	vogue	plage	plague						
> begile	beguile	fuge	fugue	broge	brogue						
> cataloge	catalogue	epiloge	epilogue	prologe	prologue						
> demagoge	demagogue	synagoge	synagogue	monologe	monologue						
> gorg	George	georg	gorge	georging	gorging						
> Ginness	Guinness	biscit	biscuit	circit	circuit						
> bage	badge	gruge	grudge	wege	wedge						
> juge	judge	gaget	gadget	nuge	nudge						
> loge	lodge	brige	bridge	hege	hedge						

Coach: Make sure that **you** are familiar with the rules! Practice this exercise before you start!

Coach

The Final le

Unfortunately, certain lexicographers mangled many words imported from French and other sources to suit English tastes and in doing so mangled the rules! Most words, when using '**le**' need two **consonants** between the first vowel and the '**le**' to keep the **vowel sound**:

p**add** le   k**ett** le   sk**itt** le   b**obb** le   r**ubb** le

Words such as 'm**ang**le' and '**ang**le' already have two **consonants** before the '**le**'. Make sure you are familiar with the sound before you start.

If you wish the vowel to say its **name** then do not double the **consonant**:

t**ab**le tr**if**le n**ob**le b**ug**le.

Demonstrate the '**le**' ending on scrap paper and start the exercise.

Note: The last four words in **column 4** have French origins: **double**, **trouble**, **couple**, **touch**, and they have to be taught as exceptions to the rules. The colour coding demonstrates the English pronunciation. However, the sound is subject to regional variations.

Follow the column guides. Speak clearly.

Day		beware *	Day		beware *	Day		Day	
Month			Month			Month		Month	
Pro			Pro			Spell		Spell	
kettle			gentle			*grapple*		*spangle*	
raffle			angle			*hobble*		*tangle*	
gifted *			dangle			*rubble*		*chortle*	
giggle *			handle			*paddle*		*goggle*	
muddle			subtle			*middle*		*bundle*	
begin *			uncle			*bottle*		*swindle*	
saddle			single			*shuttle*		*struggle*	
forgive *			mingle			*shuffle*		*bangle*	
stubble			touch *			*riddle*		*double*	
throttle			trouble			*hassle*		*trouble*	
quibble			couple			*supple*		*couple*	
apple			double			*juggle*		*touch*	

Coach: Two **consonants** must be used before an 'le' ending for the vowel to say its **sound**: pu**dd**le.
One **consonant** must be used before an 'le' ending to say its vowel **name**: ca**b**le.

--

Day					Day					Day					Day				
Month					Month					Month					Month					
Pro					Spell					Pro					Spell	Soft 'c'				
table					*stable*					get					*farce*					
rifle					*trifle*					linger					*cycle*					
bible					*entitle*					anger					*entice*					
bugle					*unstable*					bigger					*device*					
noble					*ignoble*					girl					*vicinity*					
enable					*thistle*					forget					*cinder*					
disable					*uncle*					forgive					*force*					
maple					*bungle*					gift					*brace*					
sable					*sample*					banger					*ounce*					
cable					*strangle*					given					*bounce*					
title					*jingle*					begin					*trounce*					
staple					*bugle*					girdle					*prince*					
soluble					*gargle*					longer					*cider*					
stifle					*tingle*					girder					*mercy*					

Read and Pronounce

The trouble with 'double' and 'couple' is the vowel combination 'ou'. To some people in the North it might seem to have a surplus 'o'. However, some people in the South might think that the 'u' was unnecessary. It's all quite a muddle. Play a fiddle; solve a riddle; saddle a horse; step over a puddle; stay free and single; marry and mingle. Coins jingle; nerves jangle; families squabble; dust settles; kettles boil; nettles sting; skittles fall; Tarzan swings through the jungle; dyslexics' spellings are in a muddle; but The Word Wasp helps them with their struggle. Thread a needle; hold a handle; try to avoid the deepest puddles; or you may find that your ankles are soaking wet and you must dangle them above the fire (in the absence of a mangle). Percy and Cecil were friends of both Cynthia and Gerry who had just moved to the centre of the city. High above the ridge and beyond the hedge; far from the village and under a ledge; a badger took a lodger into her lodge and little did the council know: she had ten more lodgers down below! You must announce to the crowd that a bouncing baby girl has been born and she weighs seven pounds and eight ounces. It is possible; indeed probable, that some vegetables might not be edible before cooking.

Coach

The Diphthongs au and aw

Ask your student to listen to the following sounds:

au in the word haunt
aw in the word law

Don't forget to stress both parts of the word '**because**' in the spelling columns:

be-cause and not **bi-coz!**

Your student must hear the 'au' saying 'or'!

Follow the column guides. Speak clearly.

Day				au = or		Day		ghost *		Day		
Month						Month				Month		
Pro						Spell				Spell		
Paul	cause	vaunted				cause				trundle		
maul	because	jaunt				because				kettle		
August	pause	launder				exhaust				strangle		
launch	audit	nautical				launch				autonomy		
fraud	gaudy	applaud				haunt				grudge		
taunt	laundry	exhaust				taught *				bridge		
gaunt	flaunt	fauna				trauma				bandage		
saunter	haul	maraud				August				angle		
daunted	haulage	debauch				haulage				haunches		
haunt	autism	caustic				laundry				gaudy		
haunted	staunch	trauma				taunt				budge		
austere	defraud	taught				defraud				middle		

Day			aw = or	Day		aw	Day		aw
Month				**Month**			**Month**		
Pro				Spell			Spell		
saw	jigsaw	prawn		*yawning*			*yawned*		
sawn	withdraw	spawn		*withdraw*			*awning*		
paw	drawn	awful		*thawing*			*dawned*		
outlaw	crawl	lawful		*scrawny*			*evidence*		
draw	crawling	brawl		*awful*			*trounce*		
claw	sprawl	shawl		*hawthorn*			*bugle*		
fawn	dawn	Dawson		*sprawling*			*scruple*		
straw	drawing	awning		*trawled*			*shawl*		
jackdaw	trawler	bradawl		*tawny*			*double*		
lawn	hawk	tawdry		*lawfully*			*couple*		
Crawford	yawning	pawn		*vaunted*			*trouble*		
sawdust	bawdy	flawed		*squawks*			*touch*		

Read and Pronounce
A Shell Guide to Sandy Places

In sandy places far away

children might be seen to play

gathering shells for their displays in gardens.

Often, by misfortune, led astray

on their legs by the end of the day,

a painting in oil and sand

with mother there on hand

to clean away the crude.

But then, on some other day, fresh and

sweet, without a care, a child might

travel there and collect more shells

to use as currency:

A sweet, a bike ride or a borrowed ball

paid for by a razor shell and yet,

in some sandy place, far away,

a child might be seen to play:

gathering shells

clustered round a village well.

The seedlings of hell as parachutes

fell on the playground as wisps

of willow herb. The price of oil

is rising, so we are told.

In a sandy place far away,

children can be seen to play

gathering shells and dying.

Often forced, but rarely led astray,

as the wells increase their flow

nothing on their stumps to show

but bloody bandages.

So do take care when collecting shells,

the crude tanker's careless spillage

can pollute the beach of a coastal village

and in those deserts far away

bring hell to work and hell to play.

Read and Pronounce

The image of the Common Wasp, Vespula Vulgaris, is generally bad. They are at their worst in late autumn. When the breeding season is over, swarms of redundant males gather round dustbins or anywhere that can supply an easily available source of food. It's as if they are having one last binge before they die. However, there is another side to these insects. They carry a sting which is the main cause of concern and fear but in many ways they are beneficial insects with a highly developed **social** structure. The queen wasps alone survive the winter. Emerging in late spring, they begin to search for a nest site. These are the huge wasps we see in our houses in late May. Once a site has been found construction begins at a pace. The nest is made from paper or dried grass: anything which can be chewed into a pulp is cemented together to form a nest. The queen has carried a small packet of sperm throughout her hibernation which she uses to fertilize her first eggs. The young are born as grubs; highly prized amongst anglers as fishing bait. These grubs will develop into infertile female workers. They will tend to the further construction of the nest and the feeding of the young. Then, in mid-autumn, for reasons yet to be explained, the eggs laid develop into fertile males and females. These wasps mate and the females or queens will hibernate and the cycle begins again. Left to themselves wasps are not usually aggressive. However, hot weather and overcrowded nests

Read and Pronounce

can lead to wasps developing an attitude problem. Wasps have mood swings!

Unlike the bee, the wasp's sting does not have a barb and it can be used several times. The spike

is a type of ovipositor (egg-laying tube) which has been modified to facilitate the wasp's defensive

or offensive needs. The notion that a wasp's sting is alkaline is false. The sting is neutral, (pH 6.8)

so smothering the affected area with **either** vinegar or bicarbonate of soda is not much use.

Use a special bite cream and apply ice to reduce the swelling.

The full name of the Common Wasp is Vespula or Paravespula Vulgaris. It belongs to the family

(Hy/men/op/tera) Hymenoptera which also includes other wasps such as the German wasp:

Paravespula Germanicus and the Hornet: Vespa Crabro. Ants also belong to the same family. Some

people attempt to accommodate wasps by upholding their role as pest controllers. They feed their

developing young on a whole range of (in/ver/te/brates) invertebrates. Invertebrate means without

bone structure. Wasps, like bees, visit flowers and therefore distribute pollen and assist in pollination.

Unfortunately, their bad behaviour is predominant in the minds of many whose paranoia will only be

relieved by swatting them.   A **new** breed of wasp, Vespula Lexica, is currently breeding in Yorkshire.

That was hard going but are you not amazed at your progress?   You can't swat The Word Wasp!

Day					Day			Beware *		Day			Rule breakers *	
Month					Month					Month				
Pro					Pro					Spell				
embargo					go goes					*cargo cargoes*				
embargoes					do does					*go goes going*				
cargo					going gone					*do does doing*				
cargoes					doing done					*so also always*				
tomato					zero zeroes					*potato potatoes*				
tomatoes					any many *					*tomato tomatoes*				
potato					so also					*any many anyway*				
potatoes					always					*lay laying laid* *				
undergo					domino					*pay paying paid* *				
undergoes					dominoes					*say saying said* *				
hero					ghettoes					*colour flavour*				
heroes					haloes					*savour vigour*				

Coach: 'O' says its **name** at the end of a word. Listen to the sound of the letter 'o' in '**cargo**'. It is not enough to extend these words with '**s**'. You must use '**es**'. Example: '**cargoes**'. The word '**do**' ends in a letter 'o' and it too requires the same extension. Example: '**does**'.

Day					Day				Beware **i**ble *	Day					**'u' can say 'w'**
Month					Month					Month					
Pro					Pro					Spell					
penguin					possible *					*pen guin*					
anguish					sensible					*an guish*					
extinguish					eligible					*extin guish*					
vanquish					visible					*van quish*					
persuade					flexible					*per suade*					
banquet					credible					*ban quet*					
languish					edible					*lan guish*					
language					responsible					*lan guid*					
linguist					couple					*lan guage*					
linguistic					double					*lin guist*					
sanguine					trouble					*lin guistic*					
frequent					people					*frequent*					

Coach: 'u' and 'w' sometimes represent the same sound. Listen to the sound made by the letter 'u' in the word '**penguin**'. Write both the correct and misspelled word on scrap-paper: penguin - pengwin and demonstrate the action of the letter 'u'. '**Penguin**' is the proper spelling but both sound alike.

Day							Day								Day						
Month							Month								Month						
Spell							Pro								Pro						
people							audit	flawless								weather						
couple							ointment	bailiff								feather						
double							fauna	awful								leather						
trouble							appointed	rejoice								feeble						
visible							staunched	lawful								needle						
multiple							loiter	daisies								rapture						
credible							vaunted	scrawl								structure						
terrible							loitered	invoice								posture						
sensible							taunted	brawl								flavoured						
edible							caught	avoided								coloured						
possible							taught	autumnal								honoured						
flexible							distraught	choice								savoured						

Read and Pronounce - Watch for the ghost!

Claude Dawson was hauled before the magistrate for defrauding Maude and Audrey of their haul of Dutch paintings. These had already been procured by Maureen Saunders who had been storing them since August. The evidence was mounting but the guests at the wedding were close friends of Claude. This had caused much anguish at the banquet where the colourful language was reported to be so naughty that the haughty Mr. Gaunt was caught off guard. Oliver Hurst was not the first person to maintain that Maureen's claim to be innocent of the charge was not tenable. Did she conspire with Audrey to hire Claude? The boastful oaf asked for proof and found none. The local lawn tennis club was in need of a new awning, but not having enough funds, members of the committee decided to carry out a raid on a rival club. Many, if not most, were still yawning as they launched their assault by vaulting the perimeter fence. Betrayed and maligned by a highly disgruntled Mrs. Kitcherman, who was dropped from the mixed doubles team, their rivals were waiting and served salvo after salvo of stinging balls at the raiders as they crawled back to the fence. The slaughter was terrible and the **bruises** were horrible and even the President's daughter was caught by a painful thump to her rump. It would have been cheaper to repair the tears.

Coach

The Sound of ew

Listen to the sound made by the letters '**ew**' in the word 'st**ew**': They sound like the word '**you**'.

Listen to the sound made by the same letters in the word 'fl**ew**'. They sound like the word '**who**'.

Demonstrate the rule on scrap-paper then start the exercise. You must remember to pronounce the '**au**' vowel combination as '**or**', in the words 'f**au**lt', 'v**au**lt' and 'ass**au**lt'.

In the word 'La**ugh**' the '**u**' is silent and the ghost says '**f**' See the 'laughing box'!
In the words 'd**augh**ter' and 'sl**augh**ter' the **ghost** is **silent**. Inform your student of this before you ask them to spell the words.

Follow the column guides. Speak clearly.

Day Month				Day Month			Day Month		
Pro				Spell			Spell		
pew	withdrew			pewter			*fault*		
strewn	Lewis			brewed			*vault*		
new	threw			stewed			*assault*		
brew	Andrew			hewn			*laughing*		
grew	brewery			spewing			*laughed*		
hewn	Lewisham			mildew			*laughter*		
horrible	invincible			blew			*draught*		
gullible	tangible			cashew			*daughter*		
few	hew			curlew			*slaughter*		
audible	legible			curfew			*taught*		
stew	crew			aircrew			*caught*		
drew	spew			unscrew			*distraught*		

COACH AND STUDENT: Read Pronounce and above all take note!

This exercise is designed to make sure that both coach and student are familiar with the needs of the exercise on the **opposite** page. The repetitive nature of many of the exercises makes it too easy to miss out important pieces of information. The instructions for the exercises on the **opposite** page have now become part of the pronunciation exercise; insuring that both coach and student have the best possible preparation for the tasks ahead which are much easier than you might think. We make the sound normally associated with the letters '**sh**' in many words but most of them are not spelled using '**sh**'. There is a very tight code which you will learn by following the instructions over the next few pages.

Reminder: You can assist your student with words in grey print.

Exercise A. The yellow example section shows the letters that form the '**sh**' sound.
A tick has been placed under the letters that combine to form the sound. **Check now!**
In the white section the student is invited to tick the boxes under the '**sh**' sound.
The (**3**) indicates that there are three elements saying '**sh**' to be ticked. **Do this now!**

Exercise B. The letters '**ti**' followed by a vowel, usually an '**o**', are the most common way to form the '**sh**' sound: '**ti**' plus a vowel says '**sh**': men**ti**on, pa**ti**ent, na**ti**on. In almost every word formed this way, the vowel remains silent but active and declares: '**ti**' says '**sh**'.
Look for '**ti**' followed by a vowel; mark it and say '**sh**'.

Exercise A

t	u	j	n	p	s	h	o	l	f	t	i	m	s	h	a	d	t	i	v	s	h	o	n	g	l
					/	/							/	/						/	/				

Example Above

s	h	o	l	k	i	t	h	s	o	s	h	i	l	d	r	s	h	f	j	o	s	s	o	h	p

find and tick the sh sounds   (3)

Exercise B

t	i	p	u	m	t	i	o	l	p	t	i	e	k	p	t	i	o	m	l	t	i	s	t	i	o
			/	/	←					/	/	←			/	/	←						/	/	←

Example Above

p	t	t	i	o	l	t	i	a	t	i	o	t	i	g	t	i	o	k	t	i	e	n	t	i	m

'ti' followed by a vowel says 'sh' - Find and tick the 'sh' sounds   (5)

Coach

The Suffix **tion**

Listen to the sound made by the bold letters in the word 'men**tion**'.

You will hear that sound in many words and there are many ways to spell that sound but by far the most common is when the vowel '**o**' points to the '**ti**' and indicates that the letters are saying '**sh**':

tio**n** = **sh**o**n** : the '**o**' is unstressed (sh'n).

In the **Pro** column, all the sounds and words in each line must be pronounced correctly to gain a tick.

Follow the column guides. Speak clearly.

Day							Day							Day						
Month							Month							Month						
Pro	**sound** *						Spell							Spell						
tion* **ation*** n**ation**							nation							selection						
tion* **otion*** n**otion**							station							production						
l**otion** p**otion** ac**tion**							notion							infection						
sec**tion** frac**tion**							motion							instruction						
suc**tion** trac**tion**							section							construction						
dev**o**tion em**o**tion							elation							solution						
condition infection							lotion							pollution						
selection sol**u**tion							action							rev olution						
prom**o**tion el**a**tion							fraction							addiction						
di**r**ection induction							edition							reduction						
partition election							condition							introduction						
collection poll**u**tion							friction							contraction						

Read Pronounce and above all: take note!

Most '**tions**' are formed with '**t**' but some are formed with '**s**' like pen**s**ion and ten**s**ion

but there is another more common sound which is almost always spelled with '**s**' and that is

the sound made in the following words: v**ision** and f**usion**. It is not a '**sh**' sound at all!

It is a French sound. Listen to the bold part of the following words: vi **sion**, colli **sion**.

Say that sound now: '**sion**'!

The Word Wasp calls that sound '**hard sh**'.

When you hear that sound you will **know** that it is spelled using '**si**' followed by a vowel.

You will soon be able to spell words like, eva**sion**, deci**sion**, ver**sion**, confu**sion**, infu**sion**,

immer**sion**, as well as divi**sion**, inva**sion**, **Asian**, Malay**sian**, corro**sion** and explo**sion**.

The one excep**tion** **known** by the authors is the word equa**tion**.

Look at the example on the opposite page and complete the exercises beneath them.

'**si**' followed by a **vowel** can say **hard 'sh'** as in vi**sion** or A**sian**:

Find, tick and say the sound of the hard sh.

Example

s	i	o	d	p	s	o	i	s	p	s	i	o	f	g	i	l	s	i	o	s	i	a	j	s	t
/	/	←								/	/	←					/	/	←	/	/	←			

Find, tick and say the sound of the hard sh.

7 only

s	i	o	t	d	s	i	o	t	p	h	s	i	a	n	s	i	m	n	s	o	i	p	s	o	i

s	a	i	l	d	s	i	o	t	a	s	i	o	p	p	s	i	o	p	s	o	i	s	i	a	l

'**si**' or '**ti**' followed by a **vowel** can say **soft 'sh'** as in pen**sion**, na**tion** or par**tial**:

Find, tick and say the sound of the soft sh.

4 only

t	i	a	s	s	o	i	s	i	o	p	s	o	i	t	t	i	a	j	t	s	i	o	l	s	l

Day						Day						Day					
Month						Month						Month					
Pro						Spell						Spell					
vi**sion** televi**sion**						*vision*						*precision*					
invade inva**sion**						*provision*						*conclude*					
explode explo**sion**						*invasion*						*conclusion*					
incision deci**sion**						*profusion*						*version*					
divide divi**sion**						*explosion*						*conversion*					
include inclu**sion**						*inclusion*						*verge*					
exclude exclu**sion**						*corrosion*						*verger*					
provide provi**sion**						*exclusion*						*merge*					
fuse fu**sion**						*decision*						*merger*					
confuse confu**sion**						*confusion*						*occasion*					
deride deri**sion**						*incision*						*ad hesion*					
revise revi**sion**						*revision*						*Caucasian*					

Coach: Listen to the sound of '**sion**' in 'vi**sion**'; it has a hard '**sh**' sound. Demonstrate the sound on scrap-paper and begin the exercise. Both words in the **Pro** column must be read correctly to earn a tick.

Day				Day				Day			
Month				Month				Month			
Pro	soft sion			Spell	soft sion			Spell	hard sion		
compress				oppress				abrasion			
compression				oppression				excursion			
express				mission				illusion			
expression				commission				aversion			
passion				permission				diffusion			
compassion				tension				television			
depress				pension				seclude			
depression				suspension				seclusion			
impress				mansion				profuse			
impression				expansion				profusion			
profess				expel				delude			
profession				expulsion				delusion			

Coach: Spelling with both 'soft sion' and 'hard sion': The first two columns contain words using 'soft sion' which sounds the same as 'tion' in both 'mention' and 'pension'. The last column contains words which use 'hard sion' as in 'vision, version.

Coach

Words Containing the Suffix cian Person cian

politician magician

Listen to the sound made by the letters 'cian' at the end of the word 'optician'.

It makes the same sound as 'tion' (sh'n).

We have learned that 'c' followed by an 'i' makes the 'c' say 's' (city). However, 'ci' followed by a vowel says 'sh'.

We are dealing with a person's job title which is always 'ci' followed by the silent vowel 'a'; plus 'n': politician magician

Words Containing the Suffixes cious cial tial cient

precious special initial sufficient

The words above might appear difficult to read or spell but the rules make them much easier to learn. Listen to the sounds made by the bold letters in the word 'precious'.

The letters 'ci' are made to say 'sh' by the silent vowel 'o' which follows them.

'ci' followed by the silent vowel 'o' :
'cio' = 'sh'.

'us' says 'us' as in must: 'cio' + us = 'shus'.

The rule is: 'ti' 'si' 'ci' followed by a vowel says 'sh':

station vision tension optician vicious special racial initial proficient

Example: ci followed by a vowel says sh.

c	i	d	c	i	a	p	c	i	p	c	a	i	r	c	i	p	c	i	o	c	i	a	c	o	i
	/	/	←														/	/	←	/	/	←			

Tick the sh sound 3 only.

d	i	d	c	a	i	r	c	i	a	c	a	i	f	c	i	e	c	i	c	a	i	a	c	i	o

Example: si, ci, or ti followed by a vowel says sh.

t	i	a	t	o	i	c	i	a	t	i	o	s	i	o	c	e	i	f	t	i	o	s	i	o	n
/	/	←				/	/	←	/	/	←	/	/	←					/	/	←	/	/	←	

A mixture - tick the sh sound 6 only.

s	i	o	c	a	c	i	a	i	a	t	i	a	a	f	c	i	e	i	t	i	o	a	c	i	o

Day						Day							Day						
Month						Month							Month						
Pro	sound! *					Spell	person cian						Pro	x = cs *					
cian* ician*						*optician*							cious						
magician						*magician*							spacious						
optician						*politician*							gracious						
electrician						*electrician*							audacious						
obstetrician						*logician*							precious						
politician						*clinician*							anxious *						
clinician						*practician*							obnoxious *						
tactician						*tactician*							auspicious						
musician						*patrician*							lubricious						
logician						*musician*							mordacious						
Galician						*Grecian*							specious						
mortician						*mortician*							suspicious						
practician						*dietician*							conscious						

Day						Day							Day						
Month						Month							Month						
Spell						Pro			**cial** *	**tial** *			Spell			**cial** *	**tial** *		
precious						antisocial *							*special* *						
gracious						official							*artificial*						
spacious						superficial							*social*						
audacious						commercial							*beneficial*						
mendacious						crucial							*provincial*						
vivacious						multiracial							*financial*						
capricious						initial *							*facial*						
suspicious						potential							*racial*						
loquacious						essential							*credentials* *						
ferocious						impartial							*deferential*						
salacious						substantial							*residential*						
pernicious						circumstantial							*torrential*						
conscious						consequential							*confidential*						

Student and Coach: Read and Pronounce - i before e explained!

We have seen how the letters 'ci' followed by an 'a' or an 'o' can make the letters 'ci' say 'sh': optician, vicious, special. The letters 'ci' followed by an 'e' also say 'sh'. Listen to the following words: proficient, deficient, sufficient, efficient, ancient.

We also know that the letters 'ea' can say the vowel name 'e' as in 'peace'. The letters 'ie' can also say the vowel name 'e': piece, yield, field, niece, chief. Often, we want to use 'ie' to say the vowel name 'e' after the letter 'c' but when we do this, the result is wrong. Look at the following spelling mistake: 'cieling'. Now look at the words proficient and deficient, then read the spelling mistake again. It says 'sheling' because 'ci' followed by a vowel says 'sh'! Common errors: recieve = resheve, decieve = desheve, percieve = persheve. To stop this happening after 'c' we swap the letters around. That is why we say 'i' before 'e' except after 'c'. The proper spellings of the words are: ceiling, receive, deceive, perceive.

Coach: The rule concerning 'i' before 'e' except after 'c' is explained by this passage. Students must understand why the rule is necessary. This cannot be achieved merely by reading words. The difference is too subtle and is the reason why so many people make mistakes.

Day							Day							Day						
Month							Month							Month						
Spell	i before e except after c						Pro	ti + a vowel = sh						Spell	ci + a vowel = sh					
ceiling							unction							efficient						
receive							function							sufficient						
perceive							suction							in efficient						
conceive							destruction							insufficient						
conceit							sanction							proficient						
deceive							affection							deficient						
yield							inspection							ancient						
niece							protection							malicious						
wield							collect							delicious						
field							collection							precocious						
chief							connect							atrocious						
grieve							connection							special						
Sheffield							correction							judicial						

Coach

The Consonant Digraph **ph** Says **f**

This is another very simple rule. It tends to be used in scientific words, the sight of which might alarm students, when there is little need.

Listen to the sound made by the letters '**ph**' in the word 'gra**ph**'.

Demonstrate the rule on scrap-paper before beginning the exercise. Use the following examples:

gra**ph** = gra**f**   **ph**one = **f**one   **ph**oto = **f**oto
sy**ph**on = sy**f**on

Follow the column guides. Speak clearly.

Day						Day						Day						
Month						Month						Month						
Pro	ph says f					Spell	ph says f					Pro						
graph						phone						inquired						
photo						phantom						conspired						
sulphur						photo						samphire						
lymph						met aphor						herbivore						
phantom						elephant						semaphore						
philistine						phonic						omnivore						
Philip						photograph						carnivore						
phil an thropy						phosphate						fractured						
philatelist						lymph						structured						
metaphor						sulphate						endured						
phosphate						oph thalmic						sphere						
aphorism						dolphin						hemisphere						
lymphatic						alphabet						atmosphere						

Coach

Silent Letters

We have come across **silent** letters before. In this exercise the **silent** letters have been highlighted, once more, in **blue** print.

Bring the **silent** letters to your student's attention before you begin the relevant columns.

Follow the column guides. Speak clearly.

Day		silent h and t	Day		silent b	Day		silent w and t
Month			Month			Month		
Pro			Pro			Pro		
while			debt			wrist		
which			plumber			wrestle		
white			climb			wrong		
whistle			comb			who		
rhapsody			succumb			whose		
what			numb			wrangle		
where			thumb			wrap		
when			dumb			sword		
castle			lamb			wreck		
whether			climber			wretch		
wheel			numbness			wrench		
whelk			crumb			writhe		
whale			limb			thistle		

Day		Day		Day	
Month		Month		Month	
Spell	**silent h**	Spell	**silent b**	Spell	**silent w and t**
while		debt		wrist	
which		plumber		wrestle	
white		climb		wrong	
whistle		comb		whose	
rhapsody		succumb		who	
what		numb		wrangle	
where		thumb		wrap	
when		dumb		wrapped	
whist		lamb		wreck	
whether		climber		wretch	
wheel		numbness		wrench	
whelk		crumbs		written	

Read and Pronounce: Introducing Silent k

Many of our words have Latin roots. Latin was the language of the Romans. The silent 'b' in the word 'debt' has been kept in recognition of the Roman word 'debitum'. Some words have a silent 'k', like knee, knock, knife, and know. The word 'know' has two silent letters and we can see them again in the word 'knowledge'. 'Knowledge' also carries the silent 'd' which dams the power of the silent 'e'. To know something is to have knowledge. Knowledge of how words were spoken many years ago tells us that the silent 'k' was once spoken and in Germany, where we still share many of the same words, the 'k' is still spoken. Example: knee = knie The more we know about our language the easier it is to use. Good spelling is not about whether we know the shape of words; it is about knowing the rules and structures that operate words and sometimes their history. Poor spelling cannot be improved by giving students long lists of strange words to remember. You might as well ask them to remember a list of telephone numbers. Spelling must be taught! Spelling and reading are skills to be learned together and not exercises in memory training.

Coach

The Letters ch Can Say k - c - ck

This is another very simple rule which is easy to teach.
Listen to the sound of the letters '**ch**' in the words:

chemist　　**ch**ord　　me**ch**anic

The words '**loch**' and '**lock**' sound exactly the same.
These letters are found in words which have joined
English from Greek.

Follow the column guides. Speak clearly.

Day							Day						Day						
Month							**Month**						**Month**						
Pro	ch says c						Spell	ch says c					Pro						
chrome							*chord*						meta**ph**or						
me**ch**anic							*anchor*						**ph**onic						
ana**rch**ism							*chemist*						s**ph**erical						
an**ch**orite							*anarchy*						**k**nit						
an**ch**orage							*stomach*						**k**not						
ar**ch**itecture							*chrome*						telegra**ph**						
syn**ch**ronize							*Christmas*						**Ph**ilip						
chemical							*architect*						**k**nee						
chronicle							*chemistry*						tele**ph**one						
cholesterol							*character*						**k**nife						
Christo**ph**er							*chasm*						**ph**otogra**ph**						
me**ch**anism							*orchid*						grap**h**ic						
ara**chn**id							*chloride*						**ph**antom						

Coach

The Letters ique Say eke as in unique

In the sound '**ique**' the 'i' takes its French form, which is 'e' and the '**qu**' takes its French form which is the sound '**k**'. We use the **silent** 'e' to make the 'i' (e) say its **name:**

ique = eke:

unique = uneke.

Demonstrate these sounds to your student and begin the exercise.

Follow the column guides. Speak clearly.

Day						Day						Day						
Month						Month						Month						
Pro	French sound *					Spell	French sound *					Pro						
ique *						*ique* *						thistle						
un**ique**						*physique*						listen						
cl**ique**						*clique*						num**b**ness						
obl**ique**						*clinique*						succum**b**						
clin**ique**						*pique*						**w**rite						
ant**ique**						*technique*						s**w**ord						
p**ique**						*mystique*						**k**nitting						
te**ch**n**ique**						*b**ou**tique*						**k**nave						
myst**ique**						*oblique*						**ch**loroform						
crit**ique**						*critique*						bron**chi**tis						
M**o**zamb**ique**						*unique*						mor**ph**ism						
phys**ique**						*antique*						cam**ph**or						
b**ou**tique						*Mozambique*						tro**ph**y						

The **name** of the French 'i' is pronounced the same as the English vowel **name** 'e'.

Day		Day		Day	
Month		Month		Month	
Pro		Spell		Spell	
w**a**s		*was*		*squash*	
squ**a**d		*squad*		*squashed*	
w**a**rd		*squad ron*		*squeeze*	
qu**a**lity		*quality*		*quadratic*	
qu**a**dratic		*qualified*		*knee*	
squ**a**dron		*equal*		*kneel*	
equal		*equality*		*unique*	
equality		*squalid*		*antique*	
squ**a**sh		*swan*		*squat*	
squ**a**nder		*squander*		*quan tum*	
squ**a**lid		*squandered*		*quantify*	
w**h**at		*qualify*		*quad rant*	

Coach: We have learned that the letter 'a' when it follows the letter 'w' changes to the letter **sound** 'o': 'wash'. The same applies to the letter 'u' when it makes a 'w' sound: squash: **wa**sp = **wo**sp squ**a**d = squ**o**d.

Day				Day				Day			
Month				**Month**				**Month**			
Pro	wor = wer			**Spell**	wor = wer			**Pro**	Beware *		
word				*work*				*perceive* *			
work				*word*				*receive* *			
worm				*worst*				*deceive* *			
world				*worth*				*conceive* *			
worthw**hile**				*trustworthy*				*ceiling* *			
worth				*worship*				*chief*			
worst				*worshipful*				*thief*			
worthy				*world*				*piece*			
un**wor**thy				*underworld*				*niece*			
worldliness				*worm*				*field*			
worshipping				*worthwhile*				*yield*			

Coach: The letters '**wor**' sound the same as the **wor**d '**wer**e'. Few words contain the '**wor**' combination but many of these are important and frequently used **wor**ds.

Day								Day								Day							
Month								Month								Month							
Pro								Pro								Spell							
enorm**ous**								dev**ious**								*famous*							
cantan**ke**r**ous**								prev**ious**								*nervous*							
omin**ous**								invid**ious**								*bigamous*							
ca**llous**								obv**ious**								*poisonous*							
anonym**ous**								ser**ious**								*pompous*							
amor**phous**								am**ph**ib**ious**								*serious*							
amb**i**dextr**ous**								cop**ious**								*delirious*							
obliv**ious**								in**geni****ous**								*envious*							
j**ea**l**ous**								industr**ious**								*victorious*							
fabul**ous**								relig**ious**								*glorious*							
cancer**ous**								impervi**ous**								*obvious*							

Coach: For both reading and spelling we can say that the 'o' is **silent**: fam**ous**.

The French Triphthong eau - Read and Pronounce

The English pronunciation of 'eau' is much the same as the French: gateau - plateau. **Eau** says 'o'. Unfortunately, the English interpretation of 'eau' in the word beauty, and its relatives, like beautiful, beautify, and beautician have mangled the French word beauté, (pronounced botay). As you have worked through the Word Wasp you will have learned that English is largely a mixture of French and German. This mixture determines the way our words are spelled and pronounced. Often, students have been encouraged to use **m**nemonics (memory aids), such as 'eggs are useful', to remember the spelling of 'eau'. A simpler explanation is that the French triphthong 'eau' sounds the same as 'o' also French for 'water'. When you hear 'o' in a French word it is spelled 'eau': plateau, bureau etc.

Day			Day			Day		
Month			Month			Month		
Pro	English eau = u *		Pro			Spell		
beauty *			bureaucratic			*gateau*		
beautiful			plateau			*plateau*		
beautician			portmanteau			*tableau*		
bureau			gateau			*beauty*		
tableau			nouveau			*beautiful*		

The French triphthong 'eau' (French for water) and the vowel name 'o' sound the same.

Read and Pronounce

The previous owner of the car was devious, to say the least, because it was obvious from the start that the colour was not original. The benefit of the doubt was given. A closer inspection would have revealed many flaws which would have been identified by a qualified mechanic. The clutch was very slack as were the brakes. The gear-box crunched alarmingly and the engine spewed oil on the drive. The radiator leaked, the steering was loose and the whole thing reeked of diesel fumes. It came to grief when the timing-belt snapped. It was a great relief when it caught fire. No one grieved and they were very pleased to see the end of it. The deceitful previous owner compounded his deception by not declaring that the car had been 'written off' previously, after failing to pass its M.O.T. test. All of which goes to prove that there is little honour in the motor trade. Philanthropists are few and far between and it is easy to declare their virtues when the poor are not in a position to be very charitable. Fate always favours the wealthy, or so it seems. Certainly, those people who can afford new cars are less likely to succumb to the miseries of breakdowns and minor infringements of the law with regard to safety regulations. There is a great deal to be said for bicycles and you don't pay road tax!

Day				soft - g			Day				i before e except after c *			Day					
Month							Month							Month					
Pro							Pro							Spell					
German							**cei**ling *							*outrage*					
Gerald							conc**eit**							*outrageous*					
gentle							conc**ei**ve							*gorge*					
general							dec**ei**ve							*gorgeous*					
gender							dec**ei**t							*grief*					
agent							rec**ei**ve							*niece*					
page							relief							*mischief*					
outrage							relieve							*ceiling* *					
fragile							briefcase							*conceit*					
gorge							piece							*conceive*					
gorgeous							chief							*deceive*					
cont**a**gious							thief							*deceit*					
outrageous							thieves							*receive*					

Day					Day				Day				
Month					Month				Month				
Pro	**soft g** and the **d**am				Pro	**soft sion** / **hard sion**			Spell	**soft sion** / **hard sion**			
age					profess				*tension*				
stage					profes**s**ion				*pension*				
rage					confess				*suspension*				
ba**d**ge					confes**s**ion				*expulsion*				
lo**d**ge					express				*mission*				
gru**d**ge					expres**s**ion				*passion*				
ri**d**ge					inva**s**ion				*fusion*				
vill**age**					occa**s**ion				*confusion*				
fri**d**ge					divi**s**ion				*vision*				
sav**age**					explo**s**ion				*provision*				
bri**d**ge					illu**s**ion				*precision*				
bagg**age**					televi**s**ion				*ad hesion*				

Day				Day				Day				
Month				Month				Month				
Pro				Pro				Spell				
habitation				completion				*beautician*				
seduction				attention				*optician*				
election				junction				*magician*				
nutrition				crucial				*tactician*				
selection				commercial				*induction*				
social				unofficial				*special*				
racial				special				*facial*				
official				initially				*artificial*				
partial				martial				*mention*				
impartial				electrician				*suction*				
suspicion				politician				*sanction*				
ascension				beautician				*sensation*				

The Rule is: ci - ti - si - followed by a vowel says 'sh'

Day		Day	
Month		Month	
Pro		Spell	
Christmas **ch**emistry **ch**emical epo**ch**		*Christmas*	
chronicle **ch**aracter ar**ch**itect ar**ch**itecture		*arch itect*	
phlegmatic Randol**ph** em**ph**asis **ph**onetic		*dolphin*	
em**ph**atic pam**ph**let mor**ph**eme **ph**armacist		*orphan*	
te**ch**n**ique** **ph**ys**ique** m**y**st**ique** un**ique**		*unique*	
M**o**zamb**ique** cl**ique** clin**ique** obl**ique**		*antique*	
b**eau** plat**eau** trous**seau** tabl**eau** gat**eau**		*gateau*	
portmant**eau** n**ou**v**eau** bat**eau** bur**eau**crat		*beautiful*	
b**eau**ty b**eau**tiful b**eau**tify b**eau**tician		*colour*	
hon**our** col**our** sav**our** fav**our** flav**our** od**our**		*honour*	
end**eav**our en**am**our r**um**our n**eigh**bour		*enormous*	
cancer**ous** jeal**ous** poison**ous** peril**ous**		*poisonous*	
anony**mous** obvi**ous** seri**ous** religi**ous**		*obvious*	

Read and Pronounce

Ralph, the obese philatelist, had a high level of cholesterol in his blood, a problem which he shared with Pholidoxus, the eccentric philosopher, whose whole nutritional philosophy placed little emphasis on the physical but a great deal of weight was placed on the plate. Never a metaphysical chip was seen to pass his lips without it being covered with a sauce. The flavour, when savoured, was an obvious source of his physician's remorse. However, it wasn't the grease that made him obese; it was sitting around at ease and eating gateau without taking regular exercise. Aristotle and Plato never ate a potato or a tomato. Centuries later, audacious explorers led expeditions and explorations and discovered these plants and they made a decision to bring them home. They also discovered a plant called tobacco which smells quite awful but, much worse, it has killed, and is still killing, millions of people.

It was Christmas in the pool. Two dolphins jumped and played the fool. Chlorinated and restricted; their health suffered as predicted. Elephants are pachyderms; as are mammoths too; the rhino is a relative but not the humble shrew. Although they are mammals they are not so large and will not cause a panic should they ever charge. 'Thick skinned' is a metaphor never used for those, whose tendency for tearfulness makes them lachrymose. Bureaucrats work for autocrats and aristocrats do not work at all!

Day					Day					Day				
Month					Month					Month				
Pro					**Pro**					**Spell**				
ancient					loquacious					*gracious*				
efficient					conscious					*spacious*				
insufficient					pernicious					*vicious*				
proficient					mendacious					*delicious*				
deficient					vivacious					*suspicious*				
co-efficient					precocious					*atrocious*				
sufficiency					Guinness					*guitar*				
efficiency					guillemot					*guide*				
proficiency					league					*guilty*				
deficiency					vague					*guess*				
inefficiency					guarantee					*beguile*				
conscience					guard					*disguise*				

Day							
Month							
Pro							
Andr**ew**							
br**ew**ery							
p**ew**ter							
Newhaven							
Dewsbury							
thr**ew**							
autonomous							
h**au**nted							
h**au**lage							
c**au**tion							
g**au**ntlet							
t**au**nted							

Day							
Month							
Pro		exception *					
sw**a**pped							
thw**a**rt							
sw**a**rm							
w**a**llaby							
sw**a**llow							
equ**a**lity							
w**a**nd							
w**a**rds							
tow**a**rds							
for**wards** *							
bac**kwards** *							
aw**kward** *							

Day							
Month							
Spell							
cashew							
stewed							
Andrew							
hauled							
mauled							
saunter							
qualify							
qualified							
squander							
forwards							
backwards *							
awkward *							

Other information

Unstressed Vowels

Unstressed vowels occur throughout the **Word Wasp** and there are several in the exercise on the opposite page but to delineate them with another added colour causes confusion. Some coaches, as well as students, have difficulty with these words but our aim is mutual enlightenment!

Coach

Difficult Words Made Easy - Now You Know The Rules!

The words on the opposite page can often seem very difficult to read and even harder to spell. As you have worked through The Word Wasp you have learned how the code of the language works. Now you can see the rules working in words which you may once have thought troublesome.

Vowels in **red** print say their **name**.
Vowels in **green** print say their **sound**.
The **p** in **blue** print is **silen**t.
The **y** in **red** print says its **name** 'i' as in nylon or fly.
The **y** in **green** print says its sound 'i' as in berry or myth.
The Greek **ch** says **c** as in **Ch**ristmas or **ch**emist.

psychosomatic **psych**ology

Day								Day							
Month								Month							
Pro								Spell							
psycho								*psycho*							
psychoanalysis								*psychiatrist*							
psychosomatic								*psychology*							
psychoanalyst								*psychologist*							
psychedelic								*psychedelic*							
psychotic								*psychotic*							
psychological								*psychological*							
psychic								*psychic*							
psychopath								*psychopath*							
psychiatrist								*psychoanalysis*							
psychologist								*psychoanalyst*							
psychology								*psychosomatic*							

Read and Pronounce as many times as you like!

Dear Student and Coach,

Now you have reached this point, you will be aware that your **journey** through some of the mechanisms, rules, and sounds of our language is nearly over. You have advanced slowly but surely to a level where you are in command of the language. There is a long way to go but you have completed the most difficult sections. Nothing can stop you now!

There must have been times when you have disliked the Word Wasp; you may have felt the frustration that all learners of our language have felt. You may have felt anger because you have not been taught the rules earlier. You know them now!

Allow us to apologise for our lack of clarity and any omissions, but be assured: you have now acquired the tools needed for the study of all subjects. Your struggle will help to improve The Word Wasp so that other students who share your problems will benefit. Be sure to finish all the dotted words in the earlier exercises. We have one more request to make of you: spread the word! We all have something to learn! We are grateful to you both for your hard work and your determination.

Harry and Marie Cowling.
P.S. Just how painful did you find The Word Wasp's sting? Please write and let us know.

Let your student read the following recipe before you dictate it for spelling.

Take one page and a willing vessel;

Phonemes and diphthongs;

Slide them together and stir with the aid of a pen.

Heat them with the rude rules.

Revise, remember and rejoice.

Melt the frozen sounds with the heat of the eyes.

While lifting them into the light of learning,

Season with reason

And consume.

Super cali fragil istic expic ali docious!

Good Luck !

NOTES

NOTES

NOTES